CHALK TALKS FOR TRADERS

CHALK TALKS FOR TRADERS

Easy X's and O's from a Proven Market Pro

Phil Storer

Brown Books Publishing Group
Dallas, Texas

Chalk Talks for Traders

Easy X's and O's from a Proven Market Pro

Manufactured in the United States of America.

For information, please contact:
Brown Books Publishing Group
16200 North Dallas Parkway, Suite 170
Dallas, Texas 75248
www.brownbooks.com
972-381-0009

A New Era in Publishing™

Hardbound ISBN-13: 978-1-934812-60-0
Hardbound ISBN-10: 1-934812-60-9
Paperback ISBN-13: 978-1-934812-62-4
Paperback ISBN-10: 1-934812-62-5

LCCN: 2010920585
1 2 3 4 5 6 7 8 9 10

Contents

Acknowledgments

It would have been impossible for me to write a book loaded with so much information without the encouragement, advice, and support of some very special people. Leading the list is my wife, Joyce, who for many years has weathered every storm like a real trooper. Without her support this book would not exist.

I am also indebted to my friend Jon Christiansen, COO of securities and commodities brokerage firm Dillon Gage Inc., who encouraged me to write my first book more than a decade ago.

Trading methods tend to evolve, and that evolution for me began with Bruce Steffens, my trading buddy for almost twenty years, who has spent countless hours analyzing markets with me.

Old John Sentgerath, Young John Sentgerath, and Phil Kowalski round out my "Top Five" list of true supporters. I list them together because they comprise the core of an informal brain trust that has produced amazing insights into the markets. Several of those great ideas will be included in the chapters ahead.

To these good friends and the many other traders who have contributed, I give my sincere thanks.

Last, my true appreciation goes to Milli Brown and the team of professionals at Brown Books Publishing Group. Without their care and assistance, I would have been lost in publishing this book. They made it easy and fulfilling.

Risk Statement

The information contained in this book has been carefully compiled from sources believed to be reliable, but its accuracy is not guaranteed. Use it at your own risk. There is a risk of loss in all trading. Traders should read

"The Options Disclosure Statement" before trading options and should understand the risks in options trading, including the fact that any time an option is sold (written, shorted) there is an unlimited risk of loss. Also, when an option is purchased, the entire premium is at risk. In addition, any time an option is purchased or sold, transaction costs including brokerage and exchange fees are at risk.

No representation is made that any account is likely to achieve profits or losses similar to those shown or in any amount. An account may experience different results depending on factors such as timing of trades and account size. Before trading, one should be aware that with the potential for profits there is also potential for losses that may be very large. All opinions expressed are current opinions and are subject to change without notice.

Introduction

"Money is limited, but opportunities are not. Protect the money!"

These were the words of my trading partner at a time in my life when I had a lot more nerve and a little less sense. The circumstance that prompted those words escapes me, but the truth of the statement is embedded in my memory. No one trades with the intention of losing, but the excitement of the moment, the lack of a plan, fear, and greed will wreak havoc on the unsuspecting. For the undisciplined, emotions can range from fury to ecstasy as he or she works to reconcile the sheer joy of victory with the bitter gloom of defeat.

Stock and commodity futures trading offers some of the most exciting and potentially profitable forms of investing available. Public awareness and interest have skyrocketed in the past several years. Disappointment in long-term holding strategies has spawned an increased interest in shorter term trading methods that offer the hope of reducing personal exposure to market surprises that might prove devastating.

The explosion in personal computers with scores of trading software packages has done a great deal to encourage speculators to give personal short-term trading a whirl.

It has been nearly forty years since I first started trading. In that time there have been some truly amazing changes in products, quote access, and the ability to assess the markets using computer technology. Many of the new software packages seem to have it all; unfortunately, those bells and whistles are often more impressive than the trading results.

A lot of you, like me, don't have the time or money to sift through the myriad of available programs to find out if they work. If you are one of those people, you are going to appreciate this book!

This is for real!

As you read, it might help to know that I am an active trader. Every day for me is packed full with the activity of managing my own trades while providing analysis, guidance, and advice to the many other traders who come to me seeking advice on the direction to take in their own trades. Everything you read here has been tried many times over and has been proven to work. Some of these lessons learned came at great expense to me personally. I hope this book will help you avoid that cost.

This is not a book of original ideas, although a few are included. The originality will show up in the implementation and combinations of the trading techniques and tools we discuss.

I would be remiss if I didn't acknowledge divine guidance in the accumulation of these useful concepts. Small pieces of each puzzle have come to me in a variety of ways, including books, magazine articles, interviews, a trading partner, or simple serendipity. Sometimes one part of a trading plan would be set on the shelf because I couldn't find the proper fit at that time. Later on, another concept would appear and the previous piece would fit.

When you pick up this book, you might be tempted to go straight to the trading strategies. That's okay, but don't pull the trigger on a trade until you have read the entire book. There is much more to successful trading than following charts.

My dad was fond of saying, "Don't get the cart before the horse." It is very easy to do that as a trader, and it can be disturbingly expensive. My motivation is to help you make money without paying the high costs that discourage so many who would and could be successful traders.

You will notice that the chapters in this book are quite short. Each chapter is designed to cut to the chase and is based on real-life experience. Be alert as you read because focus is all-important to your success. I wish you the best as you work through these pages.

As you trade, continue to come back to the book for accuracy and security. And be sure to let me know how it works for you.

Your trading partner,
Phil Storer

Chart Basics

There is an unfortunate tendency among market participants to avoid charting at all costs. It's unfortunate because too many investors make decisions regarding their future on a whim, a tip, or the corporate agenda of their brokerage house. Those same people wouldn't dream of making their other business decisions without seeing information about the past and projections for the future on a chart. In the world of investing, ignorance is not bliss, yet millions of investors make decisions in the markets every day without a clue or a plan. Charts showing the market's action are actually quite easy to understand, and the added value they bring to the investment table is immeasurable.

A chart picture is worth much more than a thousand words.

One of the many values a chart contributes is the record of a market's history. We think we remember how and when things happened in the past, but a picture often will prove us wrong. Charts are pictures of how a market has performed in the past. It becomes very clear, very soon as you look at charts that actions in the market are repeated in much the same way time after time. It is this constant repetition that lends so much credibility to charting. If, for instance, we see that a market recently had a strong move up, it is perfectly reasonable to expect it to have another strong up move of approximately the same size. The beauty is that you don't need to be an expert to recognize something like that; you need only to be an alert observer.

It is not necessary to have a background in charting or technical analysis to master the methods in this book. Do not be overwhelmed when you look at the sample chart. It is there as a reference and will be used just one bit at a time as we progress. A short explanation of each labeled item on the chart is provided below. Don't try to memorize it now, but be quick to refer to it as you encounter terms that are unfamiliar in the text. Additional terminology that you might not be familiar with can be found in the glossary. When you have completed the book, you should have a better understanding of technical analysis than many so-called professionals.

Sample Chart

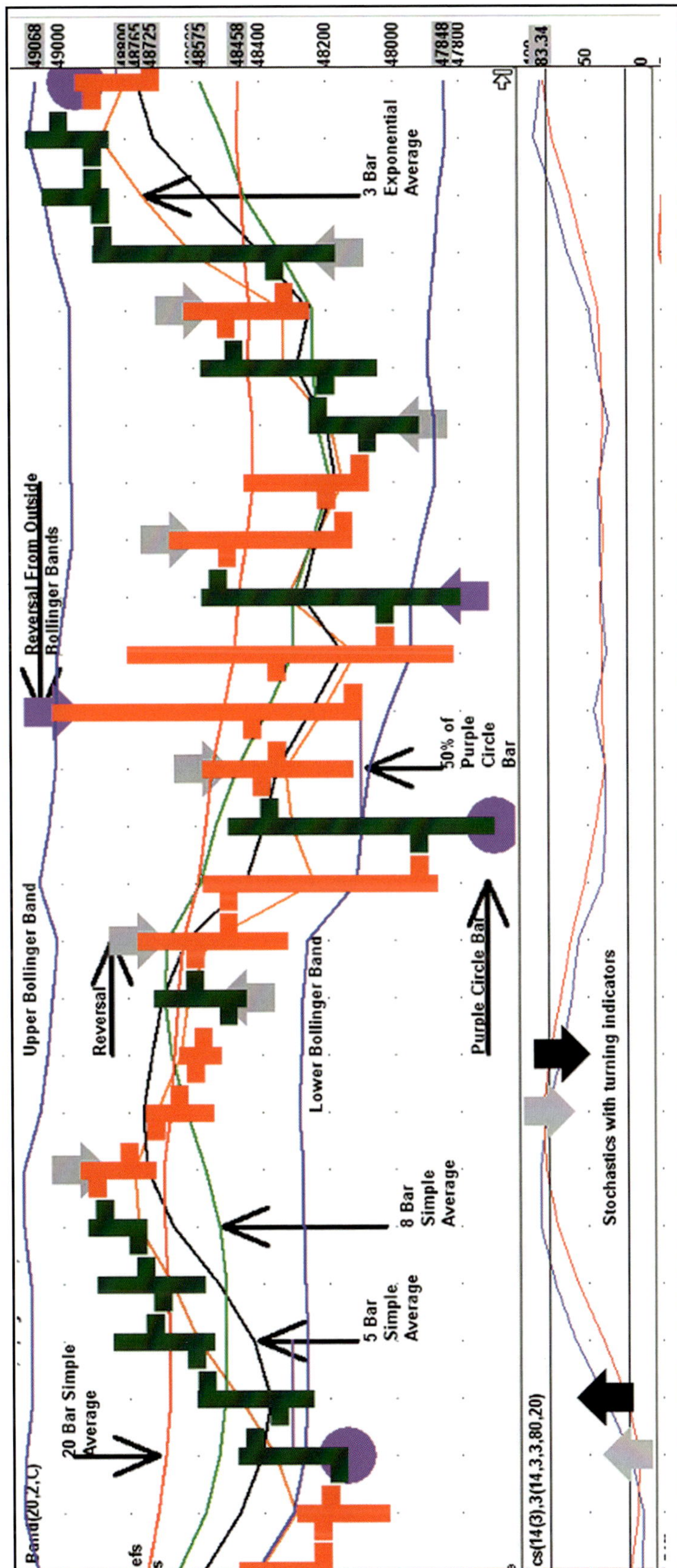

Descriptions:

Upper Bollinger Band—Blue line at the top of the chart indicating the possibility of an "over bought" situation.

Lower Bollinger Band—Blue line at the bottom of the chart indicating the possibility of an "over sold" situation.

20 Bar Simple Average—Red line in the middle of the chart representing a moving average of the latest twenty closes.

8 Bar Simple Average—Green line representing the moving average of the latest eight closes.

5 Bar Simple Average—Black line representing the moving average of the latest five closes.

3 Bar Exponential Average—Orange line representing a calculated average of the latest three closes with a greater value given to the more recent closes.

Gray Arrow—Indicates a simple reversal.

Purple Arrow—Indicates a reversal from above or below a Bollinger Band line.

Purple Circle—Marks a bar that caused the 3 Bar Exponential Average to turn away from the Bollinger line after a recent bar had closed beyond a Bollinger line.

Purple Line—Horizontal line marking the midpoint of the purple circle bar and used to indicate an expected retracement level.

Stochastics:

Blue Line—Fast line.

Red Line—Slow line.

Gray Arrow—Fast line crosses the slow line inside the top 20 percent or bottom 20 percent of the field.

Black Arrow—Fast line comes out of the top 20 percent or the bottom 20 percent of the field.

Magenta Arrow—(not shown) Fast line crosses the slow line in the middle 60 percent of the field.

On most of the chart examples the word bar or bars will represent an increment of time. Bars are presented on the chart as a vertical line and will represent the range from the high to the low of that particular time segment. All of the strategies presented here will work equally well on five-, fifteen-, thirty-, sixty-minute, daily, or weekly charts.

All moving averages referred to are simple moving averages unless otherwise indicated.

1

Who Are You?

Have you ever watched a group of kids on the diving board at a public swimming pool? The first youngster usually just runs and jumps off the board into the water without a care in the world. The next one might walk out to the end of the board to size up the situation before making the dive. Then there is the more cautious person who walks out, looks down, turns and walks back, and then walks to the end of the board again before pinching his nose and stepping off the diving board. Finally, there are usually a few who get up on the board, change their minds, and quickly climb back down the ladder to walk away.

We could be those kids, but now we're adults who trade in the markets—and each of us has our own level of risk tolerance. Some of us are speculators who are always willing to jump in first. Many of us have become investors—some of us are aggressive and others are cautious.

Success requires risk.

Quite a few of us have found the entire decision-making process to be too complicated and seemingly risky. That group usually lets someone else make their decisions for them. For the rest of us, it's important to know which category we fall into.

So, let me ask you a question.

Are you an investor or a speculator? There are some important differences between the two.

Both groups accept risk as a factor necessary for success, but investors tend to fashion a more complete plan than speculators. The result is a smoother ride through life for the investor than the roller-coaster experience of a speculator.

Speculators, or "spec traders," usually get their ideas from what they consider to be trusted, although unproven, sources. It could be a friend, a new acquaintance, a salesperson, or the media. Their response to an idea they like will be unbridled enthusiasm. There will be no issue with how to make the transaction because excitement rules. There's no issue with timing because it will need to happen now. There's no issue with risk because euphoric recklessness won't allow for it, and there will be no issue with realistic profit objectives because "the sky's the limit!"

Make a plan.

The characteristics of the investor are somewhat different. Investors may get their original ideas in the same manner as the speculator, but they will not sign on until a plan is worked out. They will want to know where to buy (entry level). They also will want to know when to buy (timing). The issue of risk must be addressed and also the matter of setting a profit objective (money management). There will be a target.

The plan will not guarantee a win, but win or lose, the investor will walk away with the ability to take advantage of the next reasonable opportunity. Unfortunately, without a plan, the same cannot be said of the speculator.

You can do this!

INDIVIDUAL INVESTORS SHOULD NOT BE INTIMIDATED ABOUT STEPPING INTO THE MARKETS!

There was a time when stagecoach drivers insisted that the automobile would never replace them. We all know how that turned out. The same mentality has kept the individual investor on the sidelines for far too long.

That was then—this is now!

"You can't day-trade stocks and consistently win" and "trading commodities is suicidal" are favorite observations made by traditional investors who think there is no way but their way. I'm here to tell you that it is time to push beyond that backward thinking.

Over the forty years that I have been a trader, a technical revolution has taken place that must be acknowledged.

After these many years of coaching traders who have a passion to win, I am still amazed by the vacuum of practical information available. We're talking about information that goes beyond theory. We're talking about shared strategies that are actually being traded successfully.

It isn't necessary to own and operate a super computer to make an excellent return consistently.

At an early stage in my trading career I began to believe that there had to be simple and reliable strategies for successful trading because the market can only go two ways—up or down. How hard can that be?

I soon found out the hard way that, without any help from an experienced and successful trader, it could not only be difficult but also devastating.

It was my fortune in the second year of my trading career to partner with a truly excellent and successful trader. I watched him make a fortune, but it didn't happen for me. There were several reasons for that.

For one, a lot of his success came from years of experience in watching the markets and intuitively interpreting their moods. Another was that he was much braver than I. What was bravery for him would have been stupidity for me. I have heard boasts of bravery all too many times through the years from traders who confused ignorance with valor—a very costly error.

My partner tried to teach me from time to time, but usually it was in the middle of one of his trades and he would become distracted at just about the time I was most confused. I tried to find reading materials, but they usually dealt with methods of information accumulation that required more time and energy than I could muster.

Time marched on. I continued to look for more useful information and gained most of it in the school of hard knocks. Some of you are graduates of that school. Others possibly are dropouts. Don't quit! You have paid the price of tuition. Now it's time to collect some rewards.

As more and more books on the topic were written, it seemed to me that most of them were high on theory and low on common sense. It was sometimes obvious that the authors were more qualified to teach theory in a classroom than to succeed in a trading environment. Fortunately, it wasn't always that way, and some authors did come up with ideas that needed to be tried.

My idea of a good book on trading was one that provided me with just one workable idea or concept. If I found one of those and I could successfully apply it to my trading, the book justified the cost.

Analyze, but not too much.

After reading scores of books, I decided to try my hand as an analyst. It didn't take long to recognize that a smart, good trader can become worthless if he over-analyzes trades.

The perfect trade seldom presents itself, and even if it does, a person who likes to analyze likely will study the opportunity until it's too late. If by some stroke of luck a market entry is made, such an analyst often finds a reason to exit long before the minimum expectation is reached.

This problem is extremely difficult to defeat. The analyst always has three or four self-serving reasons for the faulty decision he or she made. Ego is often a factor and will not let an intelligent analyst admit personal error. The cure is to build a good plan and then just work the plan. If there are losses, and there will be, accept that as inevitable and continue with the plan.

Share what you know. It helps you learn it better.

An amusing quirk within the trading world is the fear held by many successful traders that they will lose their edge if they reveal their secrets and that there won't be enough winning opportunities left to go around. That theory is flawed to the point of being ludicrous. My experience has been that teaching others how to trade successfully always returns benefits to me. It could be the deeper understanding of a proven concept or an increase in confidence or even some new insight that might lead to another strategy.

I still remember how hard it was to become a consistent winner. How I had wished that someone who knew how it could happen would tell me! That is the reason I am writing this book now. As you read and digest this information and apply the simple strategies set forth here to your own trading, I hope you will know that your time here was well spent. I simply ask that you read carefully and follow the disciplines as I state them.

Suit yourself. You are unique!

We humans like to customize ideas to fit our individual style, and I know that you will want to do that. But as you customize and modify, try to stay true to the basic principles of each strategy. My hope is that I can help you reach a level of success in trading that will provide you with great satisfaction and quality results beyond any that you have experienced so far.

As fascinating as the tricks of the trade can be, it is important to recognize that none of these tools will by themselves or in combinations make you a winner. Winning comes from within you and is built on discipline, desire, consistency of purpose, and a positive image that you constantly renew as you see yourself as successful—even when you've just had a loss.

How do you see yourself? Do you have a goal to reach for? Are you a saver or a spender? How important is money to you? Are you able to change your mind? Are you wishy-washy? Do you plan things out or shoot from the hip? Can you deal with loss? Can you handle success?

These are just a few of the questions you will need to honestly answer on your journey. It could cost you a little money or a lot of money to minimize your weaknesses and maximize your strengths. That will depend a great deal on how willing you are to face the truth about yourself.

Every successful investor considers his investing to be a business. The level of success in any business depends largely on the business plan. Trading is no different. As you study and learn the different methods presented in this book, it will benefit you to produce a checklist representative of the method you choose so that, as you plan your trade, you won't overlook details that are critical to your success.

I can't emphasize this enough. There have been so many times in my own experience that, after a trade went bad, I would look back and identify my lack of attention to detail as the major reason for failure. There are several reasons for making a list and checking it twice before entering a trade. One is that it slows you down and gives your system time to breathe before you take the plunge. Another benefit is that the list will help you to move the trade away from the emotional and closer to rational. The checklist also helps to build the confidence that fuels your success when you know that you did everything according to the plan.

You can't and won't win them all.

Let's face it. Neither you nor I are going to win them all. The important thing is to manage our businesses so that, when a loss occurs, there will be no reason for us to beat ourselves up or feel guilty about the loss. Knowing that we have behaved correctly allows us to go right back out and give our businesses another opportunity to succeed.

We deal with unpredictability continually in life and yet we go on. When a trade is well planned and still fails, it is often simply due to the randomness of the market.

In my first book, *Tricks of the Trade,* I told the story of a husband and wife who came to our office to trade. They had inherited a significant sum of money and hoped to parlay it into a fortune. Their intentions were good and their enthusiasm boundless, but their plan needed help—actually, there was no plan.

They had a common tendency that many traders—even successful ones—are plagued with: the compulsion to fight the trend. As a result, our couple continually bought into weak markets and sold (went short) into strong markets. I won't say that you can't sometimes win that way, but it isn't a good plan all of the time—especially when your plan consists of placing the trade and then praying.

Now, I'm a firm believer in the power of prayer, but in situations like this, I believe that it's best to have a plan before the prayer—a plan concerning how, when, and where to enter the market or what to do if the market moves in your favor or goes against you.

You can probably guess how this all turned out. They refused to change their approach and eventually lost much more than they should have. That would not have happened if they had been willing to work out a plan before each trade.

Find a partner.

One of the best ways to stay on track is to include someone else in your trading plan. It should be someone who understands you, your methods, and the markets. The real value of a trading partner comes from the partner's willingness to discuss trades with you in a way that helps you stay true to your plan.

People like this are few and far between, so you may need to find a willing broker to teach your method to and then use as your sounding board.

Did you catch what I just said? You can teach your broker! If you learn the concepts in this book, I promise you that you will have a great deal to teach him or her.

Remember that accepting new ideas is sometimes difficult for people who think they are supposed to be the experts. Don't worry about that. This is about you and your personal success. If your broker won't or can't work within your plan, you may need to find a new broker.

Successful traders are investors. They have a plan.

Summary

1. Find out how you respond to challenges.
2. Realize that risk always precedes success.
3. Make a plan if you expect to succeed.
4. With a good plan you can trade and win.
5. Don't be limited by voices from the past.
6. Make analysis a part of the plan but not the goal.
7. Benefit yourself by sharing what you learn.
8. Customize the plan to fit your own personality and traits.
9. Accept occasional loss as a cost of doing business.

2
Planning the Trade

When I was growing up, my family lived for several years in South Dakota. My father's job required him to travel the western half of the state to visit rural families throughout the year. That part of the country consists of a huge expanse of desolate prairie. At the time, very few roads were paved, and even if they were, you were likely to see road signs warning that the next gas station would be 50 miles down the road.

Winters there are brutal, and the blizzards can be deadly. Every winter it was common to hear about unfortunate people who succumbed to the extreme weather and froze to death. Thankfully, Dad always made it back home. That's because he had a plan.

Before leaving on each trip, he always told my mother where he intended to go and when he expected to be back. That seemed normal to me because my mom always asked me those questions when I left the house, too. It didn't occur to me until I was older that Dad had a much more important reason for giving her that information. It was a valuable part of a protection plan in case he got lost in a blizzard.

From mid-October until mid-May, he carried a shovel, an old army parka, a compass, matches, a kerosene lantern, a wool blanket, and five gallons of gas in a can in the trunk of the car. Those things were all part of the plan that would bring him home safely.

He did get caught in blizzards from time to time. One time he topped a crest in the road and plowed into a snowdrift that had formed on the other side of the hill, almost completely burying his car. It was late afternoon, and the sun was about to go down. Knowing that if he stayed in the car someone else could come over the hill in the dark and land on top of him, Dad took his shovel a safe distance away from the road and dug a cave into the back side of the snow bank, put on the warmer clothes he'd brought, and crawled into his cave. Then, to keep out the bitter cold, he scooped snow back from the inside toward the entrance until it was closed.

The next day he tried to get the car out to no avail. On the second day, a rancher spotted him from a plane and came back with a tractor to pull him out of the snow bank.

Successful traders have a plan.

The whole point of this story is that there was a well-thought-out plan, and the plan worked. To be a successful trader you, too, will need to have a well-constructed plan. Without one, you will unnecessarily jeopardize your welfare and create emotional trauma that could completely remove you from the contest.

In creating your plan, keep in mind that there are three components that are essential to every trading plan. The **entry point** is critical because it comes at the time in a trade when you will have the most input for success. If you like to be in control, make sure you concentrate on entry because that will be the one and only part of the trade that you can totally control. It is then that you can assess the risk/reward ratio so that you take a position with enough profit potential to justify the risk.

The best time to check the angle of the average line, the stochastic pattern, the Bollinger Band alignment, and any other requirements that are a part of the trade plan is before you enter the market. It is important to understand that if any qualifying criteria come up short, it is perfectly all right to pass on the trade and begin to look for another.

Remember that choosing the wrong place, time, or direction to enter the trade without proper risk management can result in losses much greater than the anticipated gains.

The **protective stop** is essential if you plan to have a long and successful future in trading. The positioning of your stop should be determined before the initial trade ticket is placed. There is a general human tendency to want to wait and see what happens for a while before the stop is placed. That inclination usually comes from overconfidence (dangerous) or lack of confidence in pre-trade analysis (also dangerous). It is important to understand that good decisions are less likely to be made under pressure, and if you wait until you recognize the need for a stop, you will be under a lot of pressure.

The saddest times in my thirty-six (and counting) years of trading have occurred when either I or one of my trading partners decided we could get along without protective stops. Traders who fail to use protective stops are little different from people who won't use seat belts in their cars.

Stops can be used both to enter and to exit the market.

Stops are an important trading tool, but remember they are not fool proof, and they cannot always protect you from loss or put you into the market at the exact price of your choice. It is for this reason that I do not recommend entering the market on a stop that is placed before the opening. Stops cannot be triggered until after the market has been traded at or beyond the stop price as the result of some type of market activity other than the stop itself. It is possible for a stop order to be filled far away from its intended price in the event of a quick move in a thinly traded market.

For these reasons I do not recommend trading low volume markets and do urge you to consider these factors when placing protective stops as well.

Although you may not actually use it, in the end I believe that the **realistic profit goal** is an extremely valuable part of the trade. First, it helps you determine the risk/reward ratio used in qualifying the trade. Secondly, it should give you a **target** that will increase the probability for a winning trade, and finally, it should motivate you to protect a portion of your profit once it has been reached.

Most traders will learn how to use the plan and then modify it to suit their own personalities. I encourage you to do that. Some of you will be satisfied with the basic trade and the high probability targets it will provide. Others will want to milk the market for more profit when they realize that a successful five-minute trade can trigger a secondary fifteen-minute scenario that might kick them into a sixty-minute winner with enough cushion to allow a trade lasting for several days.

Some traders will trade a small position for several days while others will trade a large position for only a few minutes with the same monetary end result. The high probability of the short-term target will tempt some of you to trade large positions for a shorter time so that you can avoid the longer term exposure to disturbing market news.

I suggest you ask yourself why you want to make the trade. Is it because there is a good fundamental or technical reason? It could be just a hunch, and sometimes that is as good as anything. There are a lot of good reasons to make a trade, but there are also some poor ones that you need to be aware of.

In my career I've been able to listen in on traders' thought processes as they approach new trades. In hearing their rationale, observing them execute the trade and then seeing the results, I have been able to develop a short list of bad reasons for making a trade.

Make sure you're making the trade for a good reason.

Before we get into a discussion of bad trades, keep in mind that I am speaking from a lifetime of experience—my own experience. It may seem that I am presenting these poor choices as someone else's missteps, but, believe me, I have done them all at some point and probably more than once.

One of the worst I've seen happened a few years ago when a rather interesting older gentleman came to my office and opened a substantial trading account. His expertise was in land development, and based on the size of his deposit, it appeared that he had done quite well.

He told me he wanted to trade in the precious metals markets and that all I had to do was place the orders. The directions regarding the trades would be coming from either one of two people that he had selected who would serve as "dowsers."

If that's an unfamiliar term for you, as it was for me, a dowser is a person who, through the use of a forked branch, a pendulum, or some other instrument of their choosing, claims to be able to divine the location of a lost item. In past times, dowsers were popular with farmers who wanted to know where to dig to find water for a well.

This man's dowsers, it turned out, would be swinging a pendulum above a gold or silver chart, and they would draw their conclusions about making a trade by interpreting the pendulum's movement.

I was stunned. Our guy was totally convinced that these people could guide him on to greater riches. After stating my doubts, I agreed to give it a try although it was going to require thinking further outside the box than I had ever gone.

The ground rules were basic. I was to call the dowsers early in the day and write down their directions (not so bad for the lady on the East Coast but not so good for the guy who was still asleep in California). Next, I was to call my trader and relay the plan.

It turned out that I usually relayed two plans since the dowsers rarely agreed. My trader would then choose to do whatever he thought it all meant.

What started out as a quirky and interesting approach to trading soon became very distressing. My trader was losing his money at an alarming rate and refused to acknowledge that his methods were faulty. Eventually, I told him that I could no longer trade for him.

The reasons for most other bad trades are much more common.

The most common one is revenge, when one goes back to "get even" with a particular market. The scene usually plays out like this:

The trader's rational thought says something like, "I was looking at the silver market today, and it seems to have a lot going for it as a buy. The momentum is up, it's had a pull back, and there is a low risk stop point just below."

But the trader's irrational thinking argues, "That's probably right about silver, but I want to buy the crude oil again today. I want to get back what I lost in it yesterday. It owes me!"

That kind of thinking indicates that emotion has become a dominant factor in the trade decision. Giving in to those feelings usually lowers the quality of the next several choices that need to be made.

Emotion is often unavoidable, but discipline dictates that choices are made on the merits of the method you have chosen and not by an unrelated urge.

In the situation illustrated above there is nothing wrong with trading the crude oil again as long as the trade fits the criteria of your chosen method.

Perhaps the most destructive emotional response comes from the frustration that we all experience sometimes from the use of protective stop orders. A trading partner that I worked with not so long ago was interested in buying crude oil since the market had recently been much higher. On the first trade the market moved up far enough to allow the stops to be placed in a break-even position. Unfortunately, the market dropped, and the stop took him out of his position in the market. On the next trade we were not able to move the stop, and he took a loss. Both times, after being stopped out, the market went back up far enough to have been profitable had he not been taken out. He was clearly frustrated.

On the third trade, the market began to move in his favor; only this time he acted out of frustration and did something that should not ever be done. He refused to use stops and chose instead to just "ride it out." The market turned down and took him to his knees. It was an extremely sad situation and totally unnecessary.

A related pitfall comes from an attitude that I call "pseudo omniscience." That's when you "know" (think) that a market can't go any farther in the direction it's been going ... but you don't really know.

A few years ago a couple of young seminary students came into my office to learn about trading. After about a month, one of them decided that the U.S. dollar couldn't go above $1. I don't remember what the rationale was, but he managed to convince his partner that there was no way he could be wrong. The partner asked me how far my measurements suggested the price could go, and the answer was $1.23. In spite of that, they brought in $10,000 and went short on the dollar with no stops. After all, if you "know" the market can't go against you, stops wouldn't make sense, would they? The market continued to climb, and they eventually brought in another $10,000 to cover their losses. In the end, they ran out of money at about $1.22.

Another popular type of bad trading comes from compulsion—a need to trade for the sake of trading.

Trend traders can be strongly tempted by markets that go into trading ranges and stay there for a while. The temptation is to abandon a proven method out of boredom and take a series of small losses at a time when the best trade would have been no trade at all.

Trading for the wrong reasons can destroy great plans.

Even though the losses may not be large, there is a huge risk in trading outside of your system. The monetary damage done to the account is obvious, but you should never underestimate the **psychological** toll that a series of losses can exact.

Anytime you veer away from your trading plan, the probabilities of long-term success are compromised. No one likes to admit his or her own shortcomings, but in trading, the failure to do so extends the danger period. As soon as you recognize that you are trading outside of your system, you must deal with it.

That brings me to the third reason why bright people make bad trades—overconfidence. Winning is a wonderful thing, and it is what we all aim for all of the time, but there is a danger in it. Overconfidence almost always results in sloppy performance. Sloppy performance results in losses, and losses result in stress that can intensify any lack of confidence.

Loss of confidence is probably the most crippling disease for any trader. It can show up in a variety of ways, but the most common are fear to make the trade in a timely manner and unwillingness to stay with a trade long enough to justify the risk and attain the projected goal.

If you realize that you are losing or have lost your confidence, it is important to immediately stop trading while you do some serious analysis of recent trades. Until you are ready to believe in your method and trust yourself to be disciplined, you should stay away from trading.

Bad trades can also be those good trades that beg to be made using your favorite methods—trades that fit perfectly into your trading plan but are never made because of an inability to think outside the box. The number one example of this could be the short trade. Fortunes are missed because so many people are reluctant to consider the opportunities for profit that are available through short sales.

The idea of first selling high and later buying back low for a profit can be a bit difficult to grasp at first. However, using those opportunities along with the more accepted practice of buying low and selling high makes it possible to virtually double the number of opportunities.

Trade the markets in both directions.

Markets move up and down. Does it make any sense to trade them only when they move up?

If you have avoided the short trade, I challenge you to sit down with charts from a variety of markets and observe the size and speed of market movements to the downside. You might find that markets that took weeks to move up will move back down the same amount in just days. I believe it will revolutionize your thinking.

All of the trading tools presented in this book will work as effectively for the short trade as for the long. Short trading has long been frowned upon in the stock market and has been discouraged by more stringent regulatory obstacles. That is not the case in commodities. For the commodity trader, it is as simple to go short as it is to go long. What a shame it is to see nearly half of the profit possibilities virtually overlooked. Open-minded traders will look at the chart of a down market and see opportunities to join it just as easily as they would in an up market.

In my observations of traders through the years I have seen an additional cost in failing to trade the short side of the market. It goes back to the compulsion problem we discussed earlier. It seems that those who only trade the long side are constantly looking for what they believe is an opportunity to buy. This is frequently done in spite of the fact that the trend is clearly against them from the start. All too often those trades fail, money is lost, confidence is weakened, and the search for another trade just like the last one is begun.

Most of the other bad trades fall into the "impulse" category. I call it the "I've got a hunch" or "I just feel it" trade. These are trades made in spite of the fact that they don't fit the criteria of the trading plan at all.

Those traders temporarily excuse themselves from their plans and go with their gut. Sometimes the trade works, but in my opinion, a win under those circumstances can be a big step backward. It allows traders to make excuses again and thereby move further and further away from the safety of their plan. It can become a habit that is much easier to acquire than to shed.

Resist the urge to rush into a trade.

Finally, a popular way to make bad trades comes from the "hurry-up syndrome." This often happens while you're scanning the markets looking for a trade to fit your criteria. You suddenly see something that looks good and is in the triggering process. The tendency is to jump in and verify the validity later. That's usually not a good decision.

During my early years as a trader, our company had an order desk with a clerk who took our tickets and called them in for us. My office was just around the corner from her desk, so it didn't take me long to get there if I was in a hurry. A glass partition separated our workspaces, so she could see me jump up and run to place an order.

I remember going through a particularly difficult stretch when almost everything I tried failed. At some point it occurred to me that my only winning trades were those that had been planned out in advance. The losers were coming from those sprints to the order desk.

My solution to the problem was simple. I asked the order desk clerk to remind me to take my time if she saw me jump up and run to her with an order. My promise to myself was to go back to my desk, take another look at the trade, and then walk back to place the order if it still looked like the right thing to do. The results were even better than I anticipated.

There is ebb and flow in trading that traders must be aware of in order to experience the necessary consistency to produce success.

On a recent family outing, I sat on a beach in San Diego watching a powerful surf surge and retreat. It was obvious that the people riding the incoming waves were experiencing extreme exhilaration. As soon as they finished riding their wave, they were rushing back out to catch another.

There was another dynamic at work there as well. When the waves retreated from the shore, some of the swimmers were being overwhelmed by the rip tides, which are created when the seawater finds a common trough to return to the ocean.

Occasionally someone got too close to the rip tide and was carried away from the shore. The swimmer was in danger of being swept out into the open ocean. The lifeguards were working overtime that afternoon.

It occurred to me that trading the markets is much like riding the surf. Catching a trend is a thrill no matter how many times you do it. Feeling the water trying to pull you with it as it rushes back to the ocean is a great deal like the searching times in between trades. The rip tide is the temptation to take a losing trade, and even though it happens, it can be avoided.

Traders who don't go back to the original plan but continue to slip back into the riptide run a high risk of eventually being swept out to sea. The experience can be traumatic enough to take them out of the game and create a fear that will keep them from ever coming back. An effective "lifeguard" can be a checklist. As you study the next chapter, I believe you will agree.

Both the swimmer and the trader have the ability to make choices that decide their end result. The more they make the right choices, the more likely they are to avoid the wrong choices in the future.

Understanding the risk associated with each trade and deciding in advance whether or not you are willing to take that risk is possibly more important than anything else in the overall trading plan. If you risk too much, it can be very difficult to come back to a positive balance, but if you risk too little, your account can be eaten up in tiny bites until it's all gone.

Whatever the decision is regarding the protective stop, I urge you to use one. *The success of any of my strategies depends in large part upon the trader's always attempting to control risk. Without a stop there is less likely to be control.* As far as the target is concerned, be aware that the probability of reaching your goal diminishes as you move the target farther away.

Always remember that there is a great deal more to successful trading than a plan to beat the market. It is very important to recognize that not everyone is suited to be a trader. In the end, the responsibility will be yours to decide whether trading is right for you. You will want to consider many factors, including finances, level of risk tolerance, discipline, and available time.

In both the ocean and the markets, there is enough randomness to frustrate our drive for perfection, so it's not about that. What we want to do is use the probabilities that we know to give us the edge that we need to experience the success that we want.

Summary

1. Have a plan—success won't happen by accident.
2. Qualify the reason for the trade.
3. Relax; there's no hurry.

3

Building a Checklist

As you read this book, you will have the opportunity to learn about some of the best tools for trading you will ever find. As good as they are, though, it is still you, the trader, who is in charge of your level of success in the end.

One tool I have found to be crucial is a checklist that is specific to your method and suitable to your trading personality. It can greatly enhance discipline and consistency. Without discipline, it is unlikely that you will be consistent, and without consistency, your hopes for any long-term success will be disappointing.

There seem to be some fairly common tendencies among those of us who are attracted to trading. For one, we constantly strive for perfection. Unfortunately, we are participating in a contest that won't allow it. Besides wanting to be perfect, we want to place blame when our plans fail. We usually reproach ourselves, but constantly blaming ourselves for what we think is failure is personally degrading and can lead to even more failure.

Keeping track of how each trade plays out will help you recognize that this is an exercise in probabilities set in a random environment. What we typically try to do is set curbs on the market in an attempt to channel the randomness to our benefit. Sometimes the market jumps the curb and we lose. That can't always be helped. The thing to remember is that the level of success we enjoy will be determined by the quality of the tools we use and the consistency with which we use them.

Consistency is key.

The need to establish a checklist to keep me on track became a priority for me at a disturbing point in my career. I don't remember the specific motivation, but my willingness to buckle down probably followed a series of market beatings that were my reward for a lack of discipline. I do remember that my first attempts came up pathetically short. I had read that it was important to have a list, but no one actually said what should be on it, so I missed a few things at first.

In the beginning, my checklist dealt only with what needed to be done once the trade was under way. That was good, but it left out another part that was every bit as important. I needed a plan for pre-trade evaluation. Without that it was all too easy to end up in a trade so messed up that no amount of post-entry analysis could save it.

It was quite a while before the idea of creating a post-trade checklist crossed my mind. At first it didn't seem like it would be worth the time and effort expended in creating it. I was wrong!

In the end, the checklist became a concise three-part document consisting of the pre-trade evaluation, the trading plan itself, and the post-trade evaluation.

For now, let's just map out a generic trading checklist to help you with ideas you can use to customize a list of your own.

Pre-trade Evaluation

1. What is the trend direction?
    a. Am I trading with it or against it?
    b. Is it young, middle-aged, or old?
    c. Is it strong or weak?
2. Where do I enter?
    a. Is it on support?
    b. Is it a breakout?
3. What is my profit potential?
    a. Is it realistic?
    b. Is there more than one?
4. What is my risk?
    a. Does the potential justify it?
    b. Can I afford it?

The Trade

1. What is my plan for entry?

2. Have I placed a protective stop?
   a. Is it where it's supposed to be?
   b. Has anything happened to justify moving it?
   c. Did I cancel it when my target was hit?

3. Have I placed a priced order at my target price?
   a. Is it where it's supposed to be?
   b. Has anything happened to change the target?
   c. Did I cancel it when the protective stop was triggered?

Looking Back

1. If the trade was a winner:
   a. Did I get my target price?
   b. If not, why not?
   c. Did I manage my protective stop correctly?
   d. What will I do differently next time?

2. If the trade lost:
   a. Did I get too close with my stop?
   b. Did I get out because of emotions?
   c. Was the target price hit?
   d. Was I with the trend?

I mentioned earlier that not every trade will be a winner. It is hugely important that the checklist be used to verify for yourself that there is no reason to feel guilty over a loss. If the loss was the result of a breakdown in your own discipline, the checklist lets you know what you need to work on. If the loss is the result of a shortcoming in your method and it repeats itself too many times, it is imperative that you make the necessary adjustments. Either way, you stand to benefit from a checklist evaluation.

As you study the following chapters and learn how to use the methods being presented, running through this list for each new strategy should help you build good habits.

Under the "What is my risk?" category in the pre-evaluation section there is a question that seems a bit different from the rest: "Can you afford it?" This may be the most important item on the list.

The question isn't about the balance in your account as much as it is about your perception of the market you are trading. Anything about the potential cost of the trade that creates anxiety needs to be dealt with before the trade is entered. It is extremely difficult to stay disciplined in a trade if there is an unwillingness to take the required risk.

Sound money management is a major ingredient in the trader's recipe for success. If you cannot find a satisfactory level of comfort with an approaching trade, it may be best to pass it up and avoid the negative distraction that it is likely to cause. An uncomfortable trade can distract you and easily cost you more than it could ever make by causing you to mismanage other opportunities.

4

Reading Momentum

Markets are moved by imbalance. If all bids were equal and all offers were equal, the market would never move. Thankfully, for various reasons, the markets are almost always dynamic.

If you are going to predict market momentum, it helps to understand one simple fact. Markets go down when sellers outnumber buyers, and they go up when buyers outnumber sellers. Yes, we know that already, but the concept is often overlooked.

Another concept we can't afford to ignore is that, upon market entry, buyers become sellers and sellers become buyers because at some point they will need to exit. Take note: I said, "Upon market entry."

As more buyers enter the market, the number of potential sellers continues to grow, and you can assume that the number of available buyers will continue to decrease. In that circumstance, we could expect the number of buyers to dwindle as the market moves up and the number of traders interested in selling to increase until the two groups become equal in size.

This is where the market stops moving, but it won't stop for long!

The growing number of potential sellers includes the same people who just recently were the eager buyers.

THOSE WHO BUY WILL WANT TO SELL!

The simple truth is, those who buy eventually will want to sell, but the dynamics will have changed. The price is now higher, and those who still want to buy have become more cautious. Those who bought earlier are hoping to protect the profits they have gained. In order to take those profits, they must sell. In addition, there usually is a group of traders who want to go short (sell high first and buy back later at a lower price). They tend to become more aggressive as the market rises. Suddenly, an overload of selling can appear, created by those who want to go short combined with those who want to take profit. The few cautious buyers are outnumbered and immediately devoured.

THE HIGHER A MARKET GOES, THE MORE POTENTIAL SELLERS IT ACCUMULATES AND THE MORE DANGEROUS IT BECOMES.

Since the market is actually an open auction, the sellers begin to ask for bids in an attempt to find others to buy the product or stock that they own. This is the main reason markets go down faster than they go up.

SUCCESSFUL TRADERS UNDERSTAND AND RESPECT MOMENTUM.

The single most important factor in market interpretation is to understand momentum. Anyone who is willing to study momentum will see his or her level of success increase exponentially with his or her understanding of it. There will be lessons in this book on how to measure markets for targets or goals, but without a clear understanding of momentum, they will not be as effective.

Momentum is a critical ingredient. The short-term trader can use it by following even the smallest incremental market movements while a long-term trader might study monthly or even annual charts to analyze momentum.

My preference is to use thirty-minute charts for my short-term trading, daily charts for intermediate, and weekly charts for longer-term trading.

Studying "moving averages" is probably the most often used tool for tracking momentum. The basic idea is that an average of, usually, closing prices for a series of bars (a line drawn on a chart or graph that represents a particular quantity of time) will be a more reliable commentary on the market's health than any individual bar closing price would be.

For the record, trading in the same direction as these moving averages is considered to be the most productive plan.

Momentum usually starts small, builds to a peak, and ends small. For that reason, it is helpful to look at moving averages for different lengths of time to manage the trades. The most sensitive length will give the first indication that momentum is beginning in a particular direction. For me, that is the 3 Bar Exponential Average. Averaging the closes for only the most recently completed three bars creates it. It is weighted in favor of the most recent close and therefore is very much reflective of the most current market conditions.

Chart 1

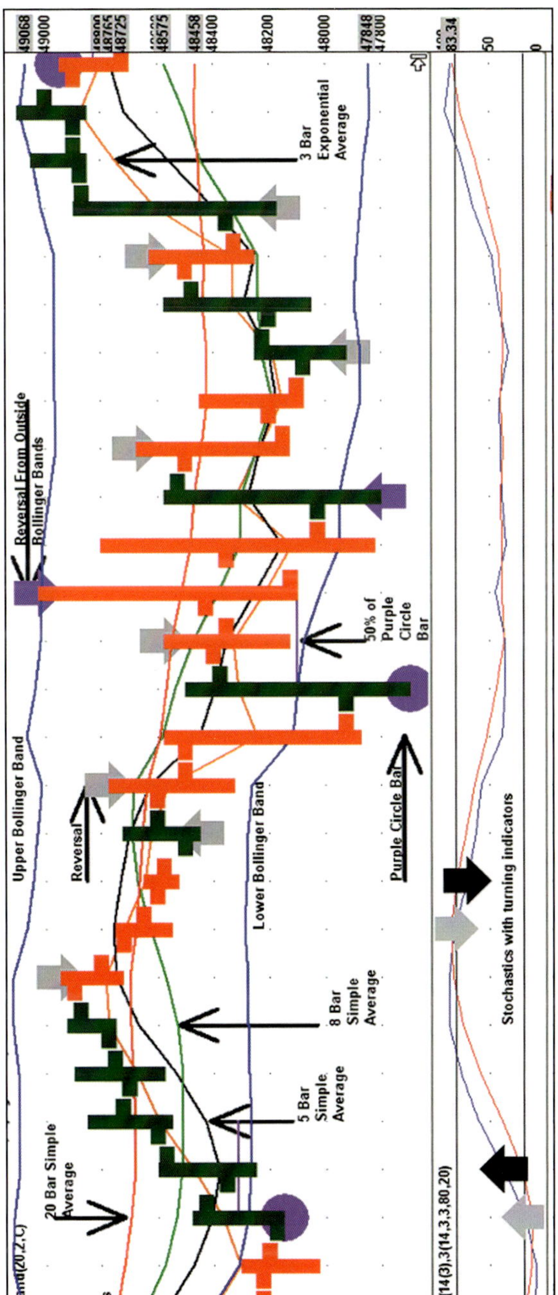

On Chart 1, on the previous page, the orange line represents the 3 Bar Exponential Average. A sharp change in the direction of that line can frequently be the first signal that a larger momentum change is pending. This is particularly noteworthy if the market has just recently touched a Bollinger Band. The purple circle identifies this special situation.

A typical sequence of events will confirm the shift in momentum. The 3 Bar Exponential line will cross the 5 Bar Simple Average (black) line. The 5 Bar line will turn in the direction of the 3 Bar line. The 3 Bar line will cross the 8 Bar Simple Average (green) line, and then the 5 Bar Average line will cross the 8 Bar line.

MY FAVORITE MOMENTUM INDICATOR IS THE 8 BAR SIMPLE MOVING AVERAGE.

The next thing to happen is the most important step in my momentum strategy. The 8 Bar Simple Moving Average line will turn in the direction that the first two (the 3 Bar and 5 Bar lines) have already begun. If that doesn't happen, as far as I'm concerned, the shift in momentum is not complete. While the 3 Bar Simple Moving Average can be used to identify the first shift in momentum, I have found the 8 Bar Simple Moving Average to be the most accurate in showing the direction of momentum in markets. For me, it is strong enough to hold a steady course throughout the meat of a trend and yet adequately sensitive to signal a change in trend early enough to protect gains and join the new direction.

When a trader is not certain of the direction he or she should trade, my advice would always be to find a satisfactory way to join the market in the same direction as the 8 Bar Simple Moving Average.

When asked to analyze any market, the very first thing I do is check to see what direction the 8 Bar Average is headed. If for any reason I recommend a trade counter to the 8 Bar, it comes with strong reservations and plenty of warnings. My best recommendation is, "Don't fight the 8 Bar Average."

Another moving average that may be one of the most popular among traders is the 20 Bar Simple Average. Because more bars are used to create this average, the replacement of one (the oldest) with another (the most recent) doesn't much affect the average. This results in slower movement of the line and a more stable zone of support, a price level below the market that could temporarily act as a floor, and resistance, a price level above the market that could temporarily act as a ceiling.

Although there are other favorite averages in traders' arsenals, I mention the 20 Bar because it is also the center line in the Bollinger Bands. Markets frequently run from one of the Bollinger Bands to the 20 Bar and then stall for a while before either turning back or breaking through for another run. A 20 Bar Average, moving at a steep angle, usually creates a very strong area of support or resistance. If the market has been moving up, it makes sense to buy against that line, using it for support. If the trend were down, the 20 Bar Average line would likely provide an area for selling by providing resistance.

Chart 2, below, shows a great example of the strength in a market when all of the average lines are on the move in the same direction. In this chart you could come to the conclusion that, as long as the lines are moving up, you can buy any one of them with a positive result. You could buy the 3 Bar (orange) until it begins to flatten out, then the 5 Bar (black) until it begins to show a loss in momentum, and the 8 Bar (green). In this example, the 8 Bar has gone flat but did not turn down before momentum came back into the market and caused it to resume its upward movement.

Chart 2

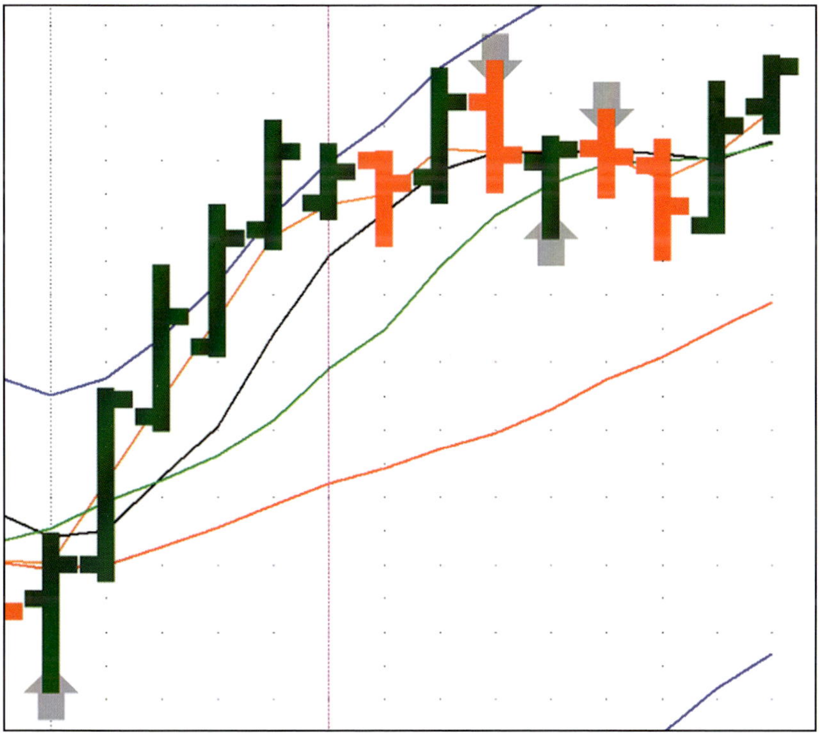

Three Entry Methods for the 8 Bar Average

I use three different strategies in joining a market in the direction of the 8 Bar Average. The most obvious method would be to go in the direction of the 8 Bar Average as soon as it turns. That way, you never miss a big move if there is one and, usually, if the market should fail to carry through, you can reverse without a great deal of risk. The tenacity of the 8 Bar Average once it has begun to trend makes the probability of a payoff far outweigh an occasional failure to follow through.

So, if the 8 Bar Average has been going down and the market closes high enough to turn the average back up, you should buy the market on the close of that bar or the open of the next.

Another excellent way to join a market that is on the move is to faithfully place an order to go with the momentum at the price point of the 8 Bar Average as it was recorded on the close of the most recently completed bar.

I usually cheat a little and place my order two or three ticks (minimum price movement) closer to the market than the exact price point indicates. This method requires you to be patient and disciplined enough to continually move the priced order every time a completed bar results in a new 8 Bar Moving Average price point.

The benefits of waiting to enter the market this way are that you will be joining an existing trend after a counter trend move, thereby reducing the amount of risk. Also, the market has a high probability of quickly resuming the existing trend on the first time it returns to the average after it turns.

The third option probably has the least risk. Once again, it takes patience and discipline, but the benefits make it worthwhile. One of the most important things you should know is the oldest closing price in the average. That's because dropping the oldest closing price and replacing it with the most recent closing price creates a simple moving average.

Obviously, if the new closing price is going to be lower than the oldest, the average will go down; if it's higher, the average will go up.

Since the 8 Bar Average is so persistent in maintaining its direction, it makes sense to join the existing trend if the market ever pulls back to the eighth previous close. At that point, the risk is minimized because on the close of the very bar that touched the eighth previous close, you will know if your position is right or wrong: a close above and the momentum goes up—below and it goes down.

These three entry methods will work on any moving average and should always be considered in the formation of your trading plan.

Other moving averages that deserve your attention are the 40 Bar Simple, 50 Bar Simple, 100 Bar Simple, and 200 Bar Simple. These averages are most useful in identifying levels of support or resistance. When used in combination with some of the other support/resistance indicators we will discuss later in this book, they can be extremely helpful.

Stochastics add verification.

There are many studies available to chartists that measure some aspect of momentum. Some are better than others, but one that appeals to me is "stochastics." It provides an early indication that the momentum could be preparing to turn. Chart 1 shows how stochastics can be a benefit.

In stochastics, there are two lines that move, the "K" line (fast-blue) and the "D" line (slow-red). There are also two horizontal lines that separate the top 20 percent and the bottom 20 percent from the rest of the field. I am interested only in situations where the blue "K" line has been in and is coming out of one of those 20 percent areas

Back on Chart 1 you will see gray arrows. They show when the blue "K" line crosses the red "D" line inside the 20 percent area. That acts as an alert to watch for a black arrow. The black arrow shows when the "K" line comes out of the 20 percent area. On some charts in this book there will also be a magenta arrow not shown on Chart 1 that points out a crossover of the "K" and "D" lines as it occurs in the middle 60 percent. These are proprietary indicators* that are just another tool for recognizing a potential turn in momentum.

This is a very short list of momentum indicators. Many more are available, but these are the ones that I have found to be most useful.

Summary

1. Market movement is caused by an imbalance of buyers and sellers.

2. Up markets accumulate potential sellers.

3. Down markets accumulate potential buyers.

Indicators are available upon request.

4. Moving averages reflect the current trend.

5. Three entry methods for the 8 Bar Average:
    - Buy when the average line turns up.
    - Buy at the average line price.
    - Buy at the price of the eighth previous bar.

5

Maximizing Reversals

One of the most interesting and exciting things to me when I'm studying charts is the simple reversal. There is so much information carried in a reversal bar that you should always look first to see where these bars are and what they have to tell about the future.

There are different kinds of reversals, and each type has information to share. The fun is in finding the key that will unlock the future. How well we hunt and interpret will affect the results.

Some of the things I look for in reversals give me ideas on where to enter the market, which way to go, how much to risk, and how much to expect for my efforts.

Reversals give us ideas, but every idea is not necessarily a foolproof winner. My approach to trading is to find reliable indicators that come to the market from different areas of study but still agree with each other regarding the direction, risk, and expectations for the trade. Some of those indicators will come from reversals, but it helps for them to be supported by additional market data.

REVERSALS OFTEN MARK A MAJOR CHANGE IN DIRECTION.

Let's first look at a simple reversal. It is the result of the market reaching a higher high than it did in the previous period and then closing with a lower close than the period before, or making a lower low than the previous period and closing above the previous period's close.

As we discuss reversals, we will look at an example going in one direction—either up or down. Whatever we learn will also apply to the other direction in the market. You need only to reverse the process just as I did in the definition of a simple reversal.

Simple Reversals

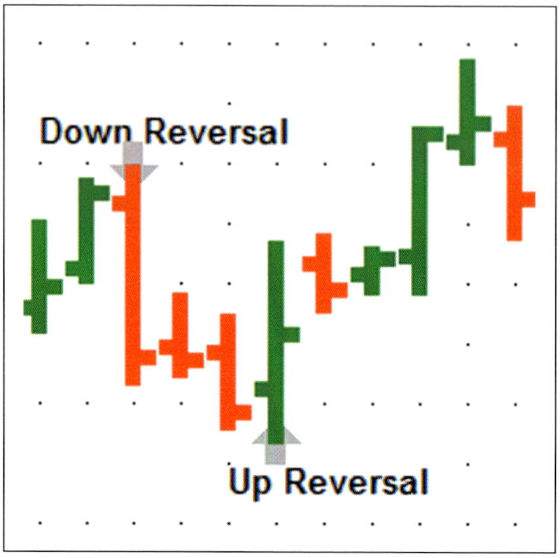

The Bollinger Bands with their 20 Bar Average in the middle and the 8 Bar Moving Average are two studies that almost always appear on my charts. That is because it's good to know where the market is in terms of momentum before any money is committed to a trade.

A reversal says, "Look at me!" but don't do anything without thinking the trade through in advance. It might be a good idea to put together a list of factors to check before you make a trade. Write them down and keep your list handy so that it will be easy to use—and then use it!

In the case of a simple reversal going up (having made a lower low and closing above the close of the previous bar), I would want to know what the previous bar's high and low were as well as what the reversal bar's high, low, and range are.

Beyond that, it could be helpful to know if the market has recently touched the lower Bollinger Band. Also observe where the 8 Bar and 20 Bar Averages are, what direction they are moving, and how fast they are moving.

It also sometimes helps me if I keep an eye on the stochastics.

All of these things can be useful in evaluating trade potential and risk control.

Let's start a list and then work down it to find out how each item can contribute to a better decision.

In the charts below, you will see that a gray arrow pointing in the direction of the reversal identifies all of the simple reversals. I use some proprietary indicators like that to make it a little easier to spot opportunity.

1. Previous bar's low
2. Previous bar's high
3. Reversal bar's low
4. Reversal bar's high
5. Reversal bar's range
6. Recent Bollinger Band touch
7. 8 Bar Average price
8. 20 Bar Average price
9. Angle of the average lines
10. Stochastics

1. The low of the previous bar is important because in an up reversal, if the market exceeds the low of the bar preceding it, there is a good chance that the reversal will prove to be a failure. This information can be useful for risk control.

In Chart 1, the low of the bar before the up reversal was tested but not violated.

Chart 1

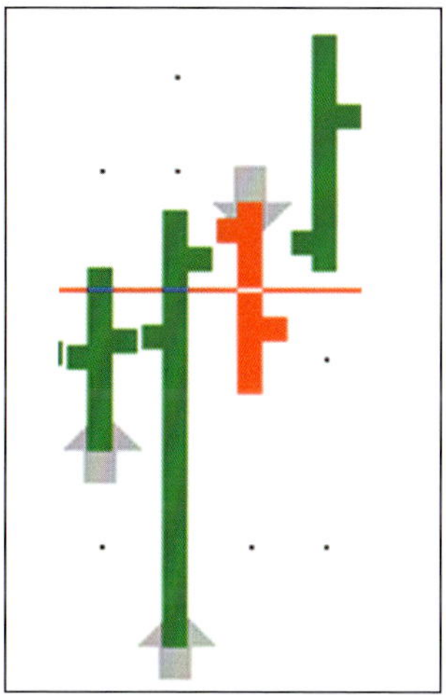

In Chart 2, the market broke below the low of the bar before the up reversal and then continued sharply lower.

Chart 2

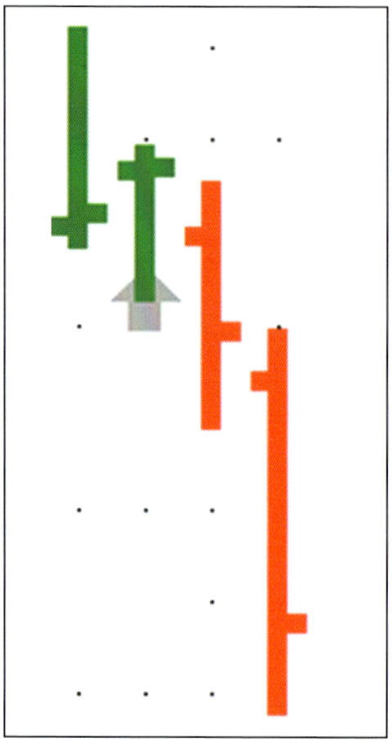

2. The high of the bar preceding the reversal is important to know, because surpassing that price often hints that there will be continued strength in that direction.

The high of the bar immediately preceding the down reversal in Chart 3 is violated.

Chart 3

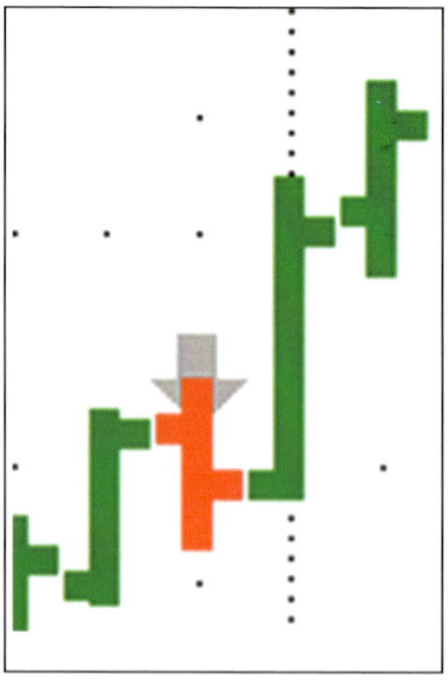

In Chart 4, notice how the high of the bar preceding the reversal was penetrated by the third period and, even though the bar following that appeared to ignore it, the market then continued on up for several more bars.

Chart 4

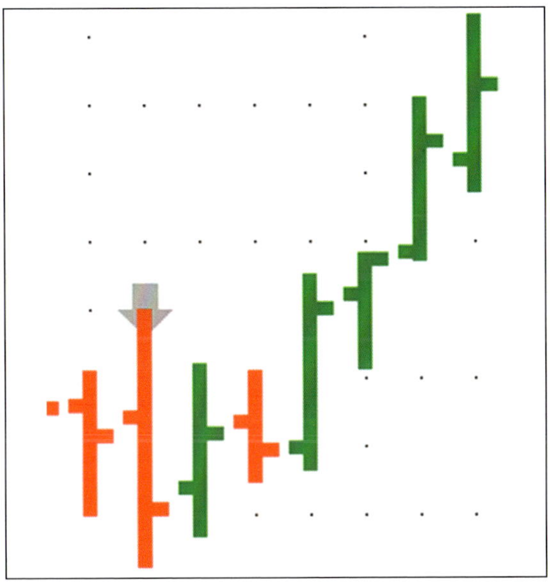

3. The reversal bar's low is a part of the bar's range. It, minus two ticks, also represents the most that should ever be risked on a reversal trade. Once that level is reached, it is time to scrub the trade and look for another opportunity.

Chart 5 shows why it makes sense to use stops beyond the extreme of a reversal bar.

Chart 5

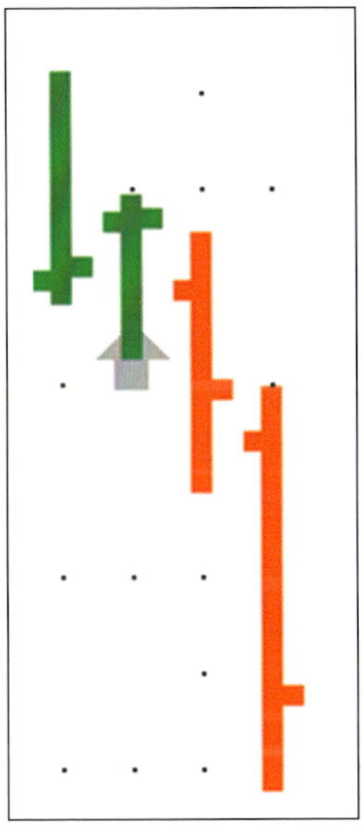

4. The high of the reversal bar is also needed to calculate the range of the bar. If the market goes beyond that high, it acts to verify the probability that there will be even higher prices to come. Some traders like to join the market as soon as it breaks that high. The potential profit is reduced with this type of entry, but the prospects are still adequate, and some traders feel that the probabilities are higher. With this type of trade, it makes sense to only risk a couple of ticks below the low of the current bar's range. The rationale is that once a market breaks into new highs it isn't likely to come back to make new lows unless the breakout was a fake.

In Chart 6, the length of the first reversal would be measured to determine the potential for the trade. An aggressive trader might have bought the opening of the third bar and suffered through that period. The fourth bar would have made it all better.

Chart 6

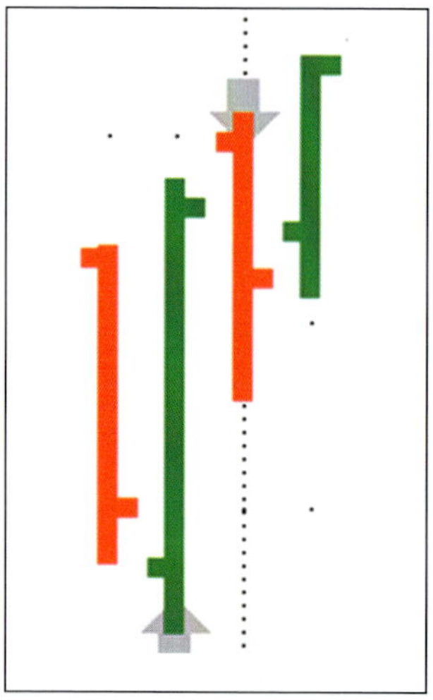

THE RANGE OF THE REVERSAL BAR CARRIES THE MOST WEIGHT.

5. Quite frequently following reversal bars, the market retraces itself back into that bar's range by 40, 50, or 60 percent. I usually wait for a retracement to one of those price levels before entering the market. Sometimes it doesn't happen and I miss out. Go back to Chart 6 and you will see that if a trader had waited for the market to pull back in the third bar instead of buying the breakout, the potential would be hugely increased. By waiting for the retracement, it is also possible to drastically reduce the probable risk. I say "probable risk" because I don't want to lead you to believe that you can always control your risk to the penny, or that stops always get filled at exactly the price you expected. Most of the time, stops are filled where they are supposed to be, but not always—hence "probable risk," but possibly more risk than you originally planned on. At any rate, in my thirty-six years as a trader I have had some really bad fills on stops, but they have been few and far between. Still, it is my responsibility to tell you that stops are occasionally jumped, and it is never fun when that happens.

The range of the reversal bar is also valuable in helping to determine a practical expectation for the trade. In my opinion, if the market continues beyond the range of the reversal bar, it is reasonable to expect the market to follow through for at least 50 percent and even 60 percent of the reversal bar's range.

Notice that in Chart 7, the retracement exceeds 60 percent of the range and then extends beyond 60 percent. Also notice that the low of the bar preceding the reversal was not violated (rule 1).

Chart 7

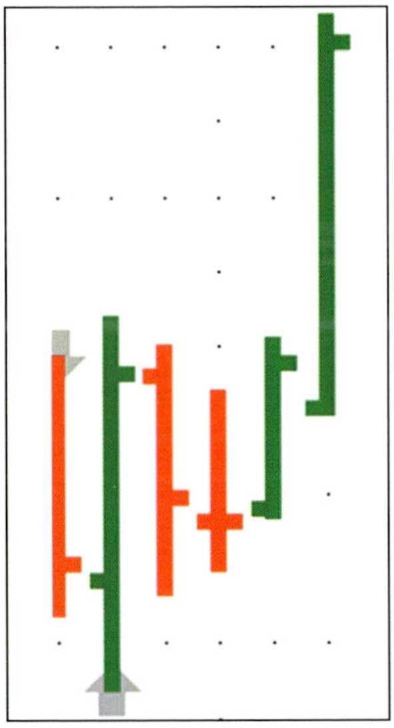

6. Because of their significance and your risk controls, it is possible to trade the simple reversal either with the trend or counter trend. Much of the time I trade using thirty-minute charts. When that is the case, the daily trend doesn't really matter as much to me, although it is wise to always be aware. As a result, it might be best to only trade counter-trend reversals when the market has already and just recently touched an overbought or oversold Bollinger Band.

Chart 8

© 2009 eSignal. A division of Interactive Data Corporation (NYSE: IDC).

Although the Bollinger Bands are very useful, you can see in Chart 8 that not every trade is a winner. However, the winners were significant. It is important to control the risk as best you can. My suggestion is to never let the market go lower than the reversal bar if you have a buy signal, or higher than the reversal bar when you are trading a sell signal.

7. The directional movement of the 8 Bar Average, for me, has proven to be one of the easiest and most accurate indicators of the short-term trend. If the average is increasing from period to period, I consider the trend to be up. I would call it a down trend if the average is decreasing from bar to bar.

Chart 9

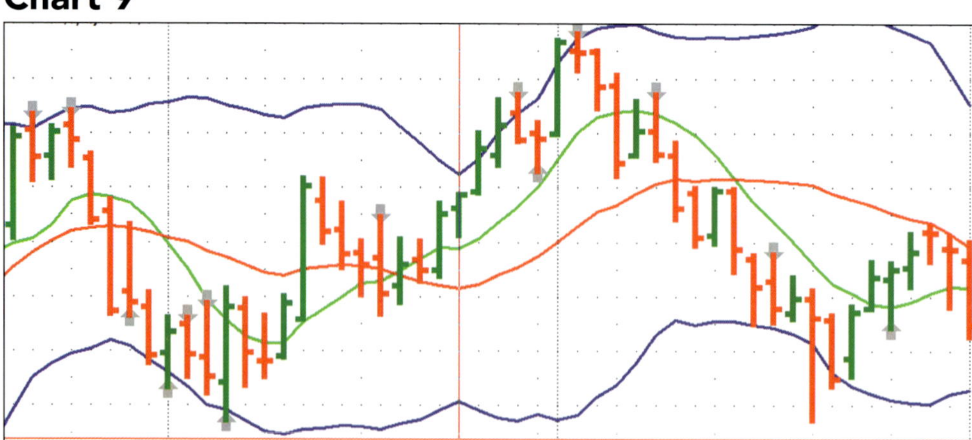

© 2009 eSignal. A division of Interactive Data Corporation (NYSE: IDC).

Notice in Chart 9 that reversals going counter to the direction of the green 8 Bar Average line, when it has a sharp angle, seem to have a tough time.

8. For me, the 20 Bar Average is the backbone of the market's movement. When it is moving down, I look to it for resistance. When it is moving up, I use it for support. When it is flat and moving sideways, I expect the market to bounce up and down between the Bollinger Bands.

9. The angle of the moving average line helps me sort out the potential trades and hopefully avoid situations that might pit me against a strong market and encourage me to join a market like that.

10. Basic stochastics have been around for a long time. It often is a beneficial tool in the trade verification process.

Chart 10

Notice in Chart 10 the stochastics seem to have a pretty good idea about the quality of the reversal.

Occasionally we see an "almost reversal." I like to call them Pinocchios because they have long noses but they aren't really reversals. I trade them just like simple reversals, using the same entry and exit strategies.

Pinocchio

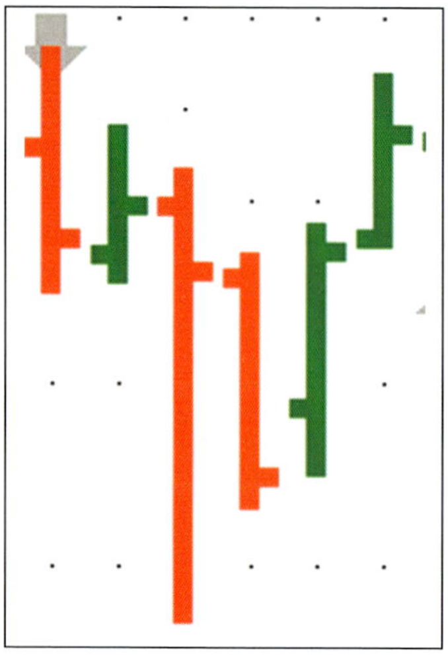

The Pinocchio Reversal is the third bar from the left.

It is my hope that you will be able to take the few things that have been discussed here regarding reversals and turn them into a profitable trading plan that fits your personality and goals. Remember, these are just tools, and it usually takes several tools to build almost anything.

Summary

1. Reversals are often the first clue that there will be a change in direction.
2. Reversals provide clear risk parameters.
3. Reversals can project excellent profit targets in either direction at once.
4. Reversals and stochastics work very well together.

6

Let's Make a Deal

Years ago there was a popular game show on television called *Let's Make a Deal*. The gist of it was for a participant to be given something of value and then offered an opportunity to trade for something else that could be of greater value but was hidden behind one of three curtains. You can envision the drama as viewers imagined themselves in the contestant's predicament.

As traders, we find ourselves in a similar circumstance every day, because to be successful we too need to make the right choices and, after we have made them, be careful not to trade them away.

More than half of my life has been spent in front of a computer screen watching the action of the markets and interpreting it for the people who trade with me. Actually, for the first four years I sat in front of a "clacker board" with a pencil and drafting paper, creating my own charts.

"Clacker board" is what we called the mechanical quote board back then. It was a complicated device about five feet high and twenty feet long that made a clacking-whirring sound whenever a new quote was generated. It had no charting capabilities. It was not user friendly.

I've seen a lot of market quotes and built many great friendships since those days and in the process found that one of my roles is to try to provide useful answers for those who trade with me. Of all the questions I am asked, the four most likely are "When should I enter?" "How far will it go?" "Where should I get out?" and "How long will it take?"

Those questions were totally over my head when I started out as a trader, so I either took a wild guess (usually embarrassing at some point) or admitted that I didn't know and often added that "neither did anyone else."

Answers like that don't satisfy, though, and it became a personal goal to see if there was a way to predict the places a market would go with a certain degree of accuracy. Later, I began to study how long it would take as well as what path we could expect it to follow. Those lessons, which I am sharing with you, taught me that all three of these challenges could be met in advance with a much higher level of confidence than I had ever imagined.

First, we will deal with the question of when to enter. Who wouldn't benefit from knowing when to enter the market they are trading? That's the reason this is such a popular question. Before we start to work on the answer, let's do a quick review.

Bar Chart Example

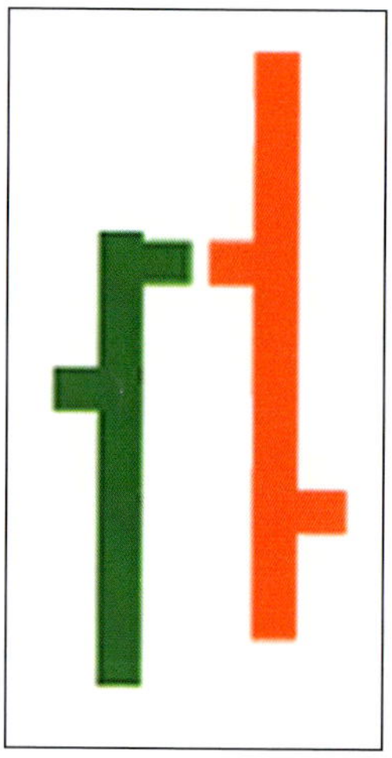

In the Western investment culture, we mostly prefer using bar charts. They consist of a collection of vertical bars aligned in chronological order. Each one represents a set period of time—perhaps a minute or a day. Typically, there is a knob on the left side of the bar that represents the opening price. The bar itself will represent the span from the lowest price of a time period to the highest price of the period. There will be a knob on the right side of the bar that represents the closing price.

This is the structure because, in the West, the open, the range, and the close have always been the most important parts of the trading period.

Candlestick Chart Example

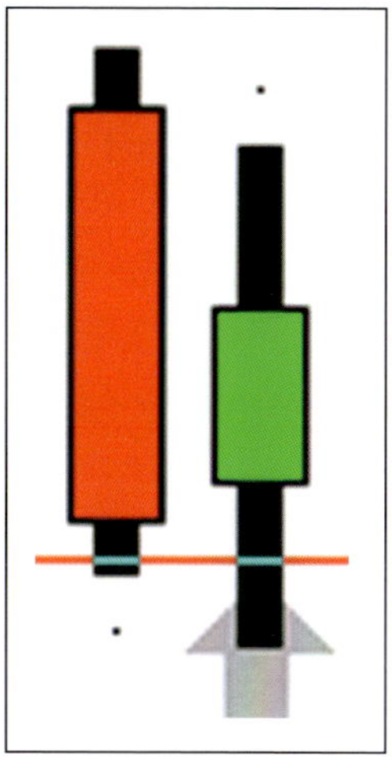

In the Eastern investment environment, the preference is the candlestick chart. The open, high, low, and close are important in candlestick charts, but the more important thing may be the area on the bar that lies between the open and the close. That area is usually referred to as the **body.**

If the close is above the open, the body is typically hollow or green. If the close is below the open, the body is usually solid or red. The portion of the bar that extends beyond the open and the close is called the **shadow.**

In my opinion, if you hope to look into the future, it helps to know something about the past. For instance, it is helpful to know how far a given market usually moves between corrections. Since market action tends to repeat itself, it makes sense to know something about past behavior.

There are many ways to find and enter trading markets, but I want to show you a very basic and effective method. Years ago I heard a renowned economist from one of the Big Ten universities make a statement that started me down a very successful path. He said that the most effective method he had ever seen in trading was to **buy the morning after the first reversal in a power move up.** My idea of a power move was any movement in a market that included at least three consecutive closes in the same direction, covered more distance than normal during that time period, and included at least one day (price range bar) that was larger than normal. Here's an example of that method.

In September 1979 I had a trader from New York working with me who managed to trade his account down from a $10,000 balance to a $600 balance over a two-year period. Obviously his trading fortunes were headed south. He asked me if I could help him turn his account around.

We decided that his responsibility would be to call me every morning, and mine would be to watch for power moves in markets. If there had been a reversal situation the previous day, I would tell him about it, and he could either accept it or reject it. We followed the plan for nine months with incredible results.

Unfortunately, since writing about his success was the furthest thing from my mind at that time, I didn't keep a copy of the statements as proof. Without verification, compliance regulations won't let me tell you how good the results were. I can say that I have continued to use that method in my trading plans ever since, and it still works. I can also tell you that my partner at that time observed our success. Several years later he won a national trading contest. When I called to congratulate him, he told me that of all the methods he used, joining the power move the day after a reversal had provided him with the most consistent level of success.

WAIT FOR A SETBACK; THEN JOIN THE MARKET IN THE EXISTING DIRECTION.

Simply stated, the system is buy (go long) the day after the first reversal (counter trend close) in an upward power move, or sell (go short) the day after the first reversal (counter trend close) in a downward power move.

I later discovered that this principle works in virtually any time frame, so perhaps I should refer to the days as bars or periods.

Shortly after discovering the joy of joining a power move on the bar after the first reversal, I had an experience that locked the concept in my memory forever.

I had bought the sugar market several days earlier, and by the time it made its first reversal, there had accumulated enough profit to allow me to double the size of my sugar holdings. The reversal day (bar) was a normal counter-trend day, and based on the closing price that day, it still left me with plenty of money to double up.

The next morning, I put in the orders to buy the market at the previous closing price or better. It was better. In fact, it was much better than expected. It opened limit down! You could say it was too good.

Back then all commodity markets had limits—a predetermined amount they were allowed to travel in one day. The idea of market regulators at that time was that limits would keep traders from losing too much money at one time because of negative news. It was a noble idea, but it failed to recognize that the limit concept created a panic atmosphere in the market, somewhat like claustrophobia.

At first I was really happy since the order being filled at the limit down gave me an excellent average price, but there was a problem. It didn't budge. After a while reality (and the math) began to sink in. A lot of traders wanted to sell sugar, but the buyers backed away because they saw a potential opportunity to buy it even cheaper on the next day.

Sugar was locked down (all sellers and no buyers) at the limit, and the original positions had given back a lot of their profit. The reality was that I had doubled the size of my sugar holdings, I couldn't get out, and at that price level there wasn't enough money in the accounts to meet the exchange margin financial requirements.

Panic took over, and I tried to sell the contracts we had bought that day at the market price. That would have allowed me to get out at the same price at which I got in and at least reduce the potential problem. I didn't want any cheese; I just wanted out of the trap!

I hoped that someone would think the price was too good to pass up and would buy enough sugar to get me out. It didn't happen.

About fifteen minutes before the close I withdrew my order to sell. It seemed to me that if the market let me out so late in the day, it would mean that all of the sell orders had been satisfied. The market would then be in a position to recover. It didn't happen.

One small occurrence: because the market closed limit down, the exchange doubled the normal 50 point limit to 100 points for the following day, but the eighteen hours between that close and the next open were mentally and emotionally brutal. I imagined all of the worst possibilities, including another locked-limit-down day with all of my traders' accounts in deficit and no way available to counteract the disaster.

At some time during the wee hours of the morning, I decided how I would trade the next day. I would put in a sell stop on the entire position at just one tick lower. If sugar opened down at all, we would be out no matter what the price as long as it traded. I don't think I slept because there was the possibility of a locked-limit-down day again—for twice as many points and twice as much sugar as the day before.

The next morning the sell stops went in and I waited in some sort of nauseous catatonic state for the opening. When it came, I couldn't believe it! Sugar opened up 60 points (more than it lost the day before) and closed limit up. It then proceeded to go limit up for several more days.

Join the trend the morning after the first reversal in a power move. Think about it! You are doing at least three really great things: entering a strong market, trading with the trend, and doing so after a correction. It's simple, and it has worked for me many times. The chart below should give you an idea of what to look for. Notice that there is a second sell opportunity on the opening of the last bar of the chart following a counter trend (up) close.

Power Move Buy and Sell Signals

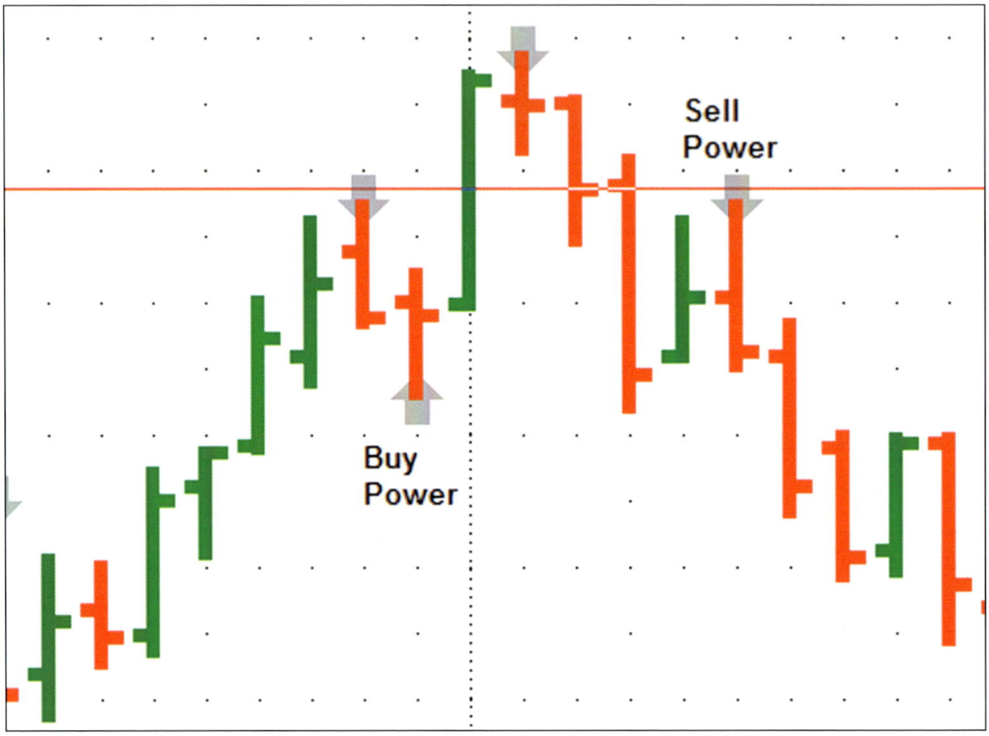

© 2009 eSignal. A division of Interactive Data Corporation (NYSE: IDC).

Make sure the market fits your rules.

As usual, even the simplest concept needs some ground rules. My rule to qualify price action as a power move is that a market must close in the same direction at least three periods in a row. Of those three periods there should be at least one that is larger than the average for the past ten periods, and the total length of the three should be greater in length than any comparable time in the past ten periods. Of course, a power move can consist of more than three closes in a row but no fewer than three.

Notice in the next chart, Chart 1, that when the market was dropping hard at first it had only one up bar and the next bar was a sell.

Also notice that when the market started to go sideways it couldn't put together a power move that fit our rules.

Finally, notice the power move from the bottom of the range to the top (three small green bars) and from top to bottom (three small red bars). There are at least two things wrong with them even though they both had three closes in a row in the same direction.

First, the ranges of the periods were not nearly as large as previous bars, and second, neither move managed to break out of the previous range before it corrected.

Caution! If the market has been trading in an established trading range, be leery of a power move that runs completely from one side to the other before it has a counter trend bar. Those can be a trap and are best left alone until a breakout of the trading range is accomplished.

Chart 1

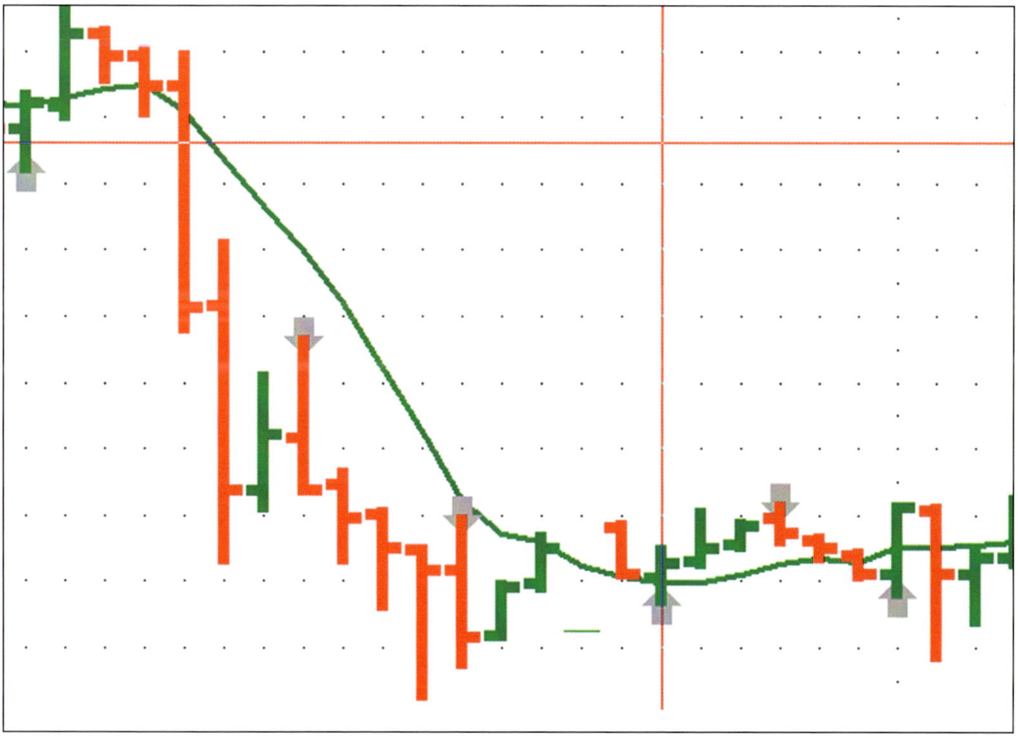

Looking at Chart 2, below, you will see a market that has been in a sideways pattern for a while and is now beginning a move that could be the start of a trend. Anyone hoping and working for a consistent level of success will find it useful to be able to identify the trend. The sooner a trend is identified, the better because that could give the trader an early start and a better opportunity to plan the trade.

In Chart 2, the turn bar is identified. At first glance, it would be very difficult to see anything exceptional about that bar. The secret is in the 8 Bar Average line.

Chart 2

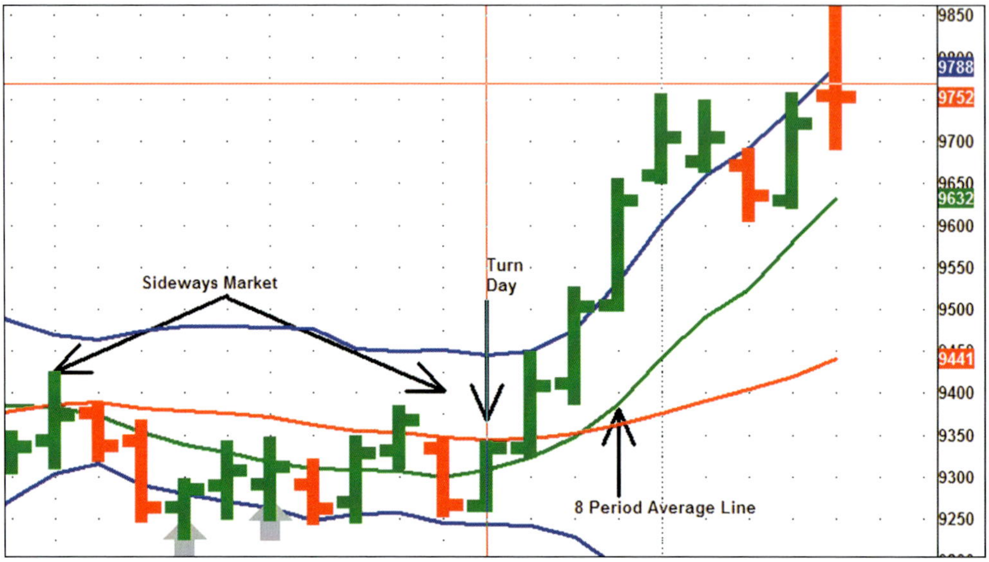

The easiest and earliest sign I've found to identify a trend is to watch a market move through an 8 Period Moving Average line long enough and far enough to turn the angle of the moving average line in the direction of the market. Once that occurs, it is okay to join the market and stay until the angle of the moving average line turns back in the other direction or some other method of protection is triggered.

A simple 8 Period Moving Average is calculated by adding the closes of eight consecutive market periods together in sequence from oldest to current and then dividing by eight to arrive at the average.

For each period, the answer is registered on a graph, and then those numbers are joined together by a continuous line. The movement in the average line is created by dropping the oldest close off and adding the newest close on at the end of every new period, totaling the new set of eight closes and once again dividing the new total by eight.

Chart 3 shows how consistent the 8 Period Averages can be.

Chart 3

Since the 8 Bar Average is calculated by dropping the eighth previous close and replacing it with the current close, it is easy to look back and anticipate what could happen. A good illustration of how this works can be found in Chart 3.

Find the first small range bar following the highest price (twenty-third bar from the left). Start with that bar and count back (to the left) for eight bars. By looking at the eighth previous close, you will recognize that, unless the close following the small range bar is somewhat higher, the 8 Bar Average will automatically turn down.

Taking that rationale a bit further, you could decide to sell the market if it goes below the low of the small range bar because that would increase the odds of a lower close and could also improve the entry price.

With no more than these two things, the power move first reversal and the 8 Bar Simple Moving Average, you could certainly win a lot of trades, but there is much more to successful trading than what we have just discussed.

Always remember these two basics:

1. Market movement almost always repeats itself at least once and frequently twice. That means that if a market moves down, it is quite likely that, after a correction, it will move down again. After another correction it is likely to move down a third time. Conversely, if the market moves up, it can be expected, after a correction, to move up again in a relatively equal time and distance.

2. These moves down or up usually will be approximately the same size and duration. In addition, the corrections often will be of comparable length and will use up approximately the same amount of time.

If you study Chart 4, you will see a good example of these basics in the movement from top to bottom that takes up the middle section of the chart.

Notice that the moves down consist of about three bars each and the corrections take only one bar. The moves down are relatively equal to each other in length, and the corrections all relate to each other in time and distance as well.

In the lower right you can see the market change direction as it also changes the pattern. Now it has five closes in a row going up. The change in pattern is often a good indication that there will be a change of trend. Notice that the 8 Bar Average agrees.

In looking at Chart 4, notice the low bar about five bars from the left. That bar represents the lowest price of the last correction made by the market before it moved to its ultimate high. We can be confident that the trend has turned down if the market price exceeds that low. That action also will be confirmed by the 8 Bar Moving Average indicator.

At this point we should probably wait to enter until the market has at least one close in the opposite direction of the new trend. Initial pull backs are usually only one or two counter-trend bars followed by the trend resumption.

Based upon what the market has done so far, we can make an estimate (with a fair degree of confidence) about how far the market is likely to go on its next move down.

It is important to be sure that the high of the correction has been put in before you measure for the next move. To make this prediction, you must measure the length of the first move down. Now subtract that length from the high of the following correction. It is highly likely that the resulting price will identify a reliable target area for the market to reach next.

Chart 4

Sometimes the market will come up a little short or go a bit farther on the second down move than it did on the first, but that's okay. The next thing to expect is another pull back, in this case a rally that will probably be a lot like the first one. Often this second pull back will be more complex, meaning that it could rally, drop (but not into new low territory), and rally again before it is ready to resume the downward trend.

The third move down (if there is one) should culminate in a "profit zone."

I'm going to guess that your ability to identify the profit zone will give you a great deal of satisfaction as it did me.

In most cases, the first move down and the second will not be exactly the same length. Once the top of the second correction is in, subtract the length of the first move from the top of the second rally and record the projected price.

Next, subtract the length of the second move from the same top of the second rally and record that price.

Using this method, you can identify the profit zone (the area between those two price extensions). The market will almost always reach the closest number and then some. Strong markets will go through both numbers, but at that point they usually are ready for a major reversal.

In an up-trending market, you would follow the same pattern except that you would add your measurements to the low of the second correction.

Please understand that there are no guarantees that the market will do anything you expect it to, including the things we have just discussed. My intention is to give you an edge on the market—not an iron-clad promise. With that in mind, it is extremely important that you establish an acceptable level of risk before you enter any trade. Place stops at that level as soon as the trade is made.

The good news is that by doing so, you can better control your risk and assess the risk/reward ratio for your trade in advance. The bad news is that stops don't always get filled at the price intended; although, once they've been hit, they typically become market orders and are filled as soon as possible.

As we discussed earlier in this book, a reversal is one thing that can help you recognize turning points in the market early.

At the top of the market, a qualified reversal bar will have gone beyond the high of the preceding bar and then closed below the close of that previous period to signal a possible sell.

At the bottom of the market, a classic reversal bar will have gone below the low of the previous bar and then closed above the previous bar's close.

The reversal bar becomes much more significant if it has touched a Bollinger Band or major moving average and reversed away from it. Looking back to Chart 4, you can see significant reversals at the very top (Bollinger Band), at the first bottom (Bollinger Band), and at the top of the first correction (20 Bar Moving Average).

Checklist for this strategy:

1. What is the direction and power of the momentum?
2. Remember that trading against power reduces the probability of success.
3. How and where will I enter the trade?
   - Buy a breakout or sell a breakdown.
   - Enter on a pull back of 40–60 percent of either a previous bar or continuous market run.
4. How will I control the risk and what will it be?
5. Always use a stop.
   - Make the market take out a price level that has been tested earlier and held.
   - On breakouts and breakdowns, risk very little.
6. Do I have more than one target?
   - Always have a probable and a possible trade goal.
7. Does the risk/reward ratio work?
8. Make sure the probable goal is at least twice the risk.
9. How will I adjust as the trade progresses?
10. Take a profit when the target is hit.
    - Move the stop to a profit position when it makes sense. For instance, when you move the stop, be aware that the market pulls back to the center of previous bars, so don't move into a price area that is almost certain to be visited.

7

Wild Guesses or Educated Choices

Trade ideas come to us from a variety of sources. It could be the evening news, the comment of a friend, or just a random thought. It doesn't really matter until we decide to act on them. That is the time the need for a solid trading plan becomes essential.

Putting that plan together can be difficult without the right tools. Until the need arises, it really isn't possible to know exactly what tools to use, but having a good variety available will give you the best advantage.

Almost all craftsmen carry with them a toolbox full of tools, and if you were to ask them which ones were their favorites, they could quickly tell you. They know which ones they use most and are most comfortable with. They probably also would tell you that every tool they own can be just right for certain tasks.

In this section, you will be given a starter tool set that includes an assortment of my favorites that will give you an edge in your trading plan. Some of them will become your favorites as well because they just fit you, but all of them will have value in certain types of trading circumstances. In many cases you will see how these technical tools can complement each other for your benefit.

Most of the studies used here are available through nearly all charting services—even the free ones that you find online.

When a trading idea comes to you, it is always important to know the direction of the trend. This is true no matter who gave you the idea. It is usually best to trade in the direction of the existing trend unless there is a truly compelling reason to oppose it. Either way, you should benefit from knowing the trend direction.

There are many ways to determine the trend, but one of my favorites came to me through three of my good trading buddies.

As shown in the chart below, add a 3 Bar Exponential Average, a 5 Bar Simple Average, and an 8 Bar Simple Average to your chart page as line graphs. Once you have that set up, it is as simple as this: When the 3 Bar crosses the 5 Bar, it is a wake-up call to watch for a possible change of direction. Then, if the 5 Bar crosses the 8 Bar, it is verification that the market is seriously considering directional change.

If the 3 Bar Exponential Average is closing above the 8 Bar Simple Average and the 8 Bar is rising, the trend is up. If the 3 Bar Exponential Average is closing below the 8 Bar Simple Average and the 8 Bar is sinking, the trend is down.

Chart 1
3 Bar Exponential—5 and 8 Bar Simple Averages

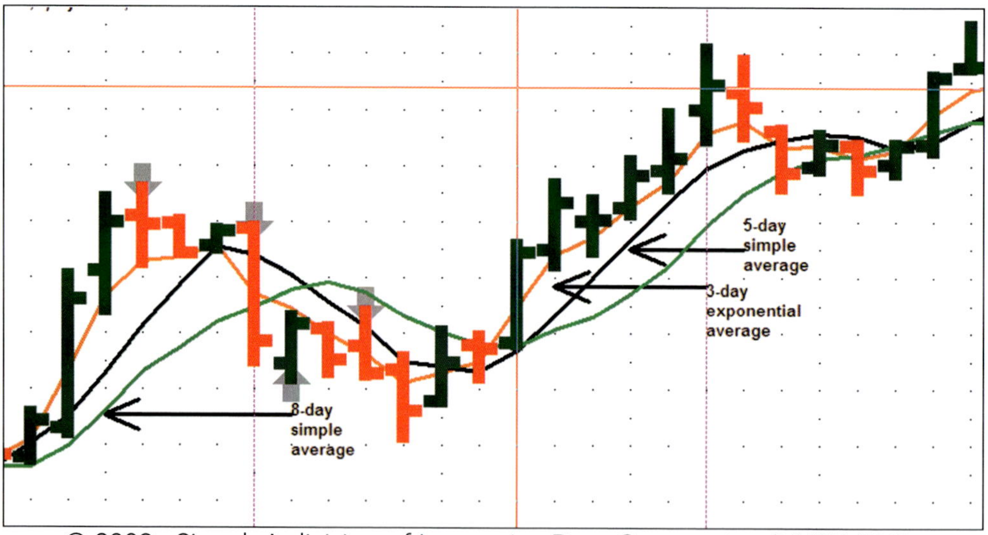

Triggers

To avoid as much subjectivity as possible while still using your ability to reason, it is important to have some triggers. These are price levels that will allow the market to decide when, where, and if you will enter a trade.

In this scenario, all triggers are activated through the use of a stop. Remember, a stop is a priced order that will not be activated until the market actually touches that price. At that time, it becomes a market order and will be filled at the market as soon as possible. This is what makes a stop order unique. It allows you to place a buy order above the current market price or a sell order below the current price. Normally, one would expect an order to be executed if you offered a price that was better than the current price, but a stop order will not be executed until the market gets there.

That way, unless the market can perform to your specifications, you will not be involved with it.

Two-Bar Crunch

For a sell signal (upper portion of chart), if a market opens above the high price of the bar before the last bar, a sell stop should be placed two ticks (a tick is the minimum price movement) below that bar's high. If the stop is triggered, the expectation would be for an "at the price of entry," or better close the first bar and follow-through on the second bar. Of course, the reward could be much more than that, or it could fail to carry through.

Chart 2
Two Bar Crunch Chart

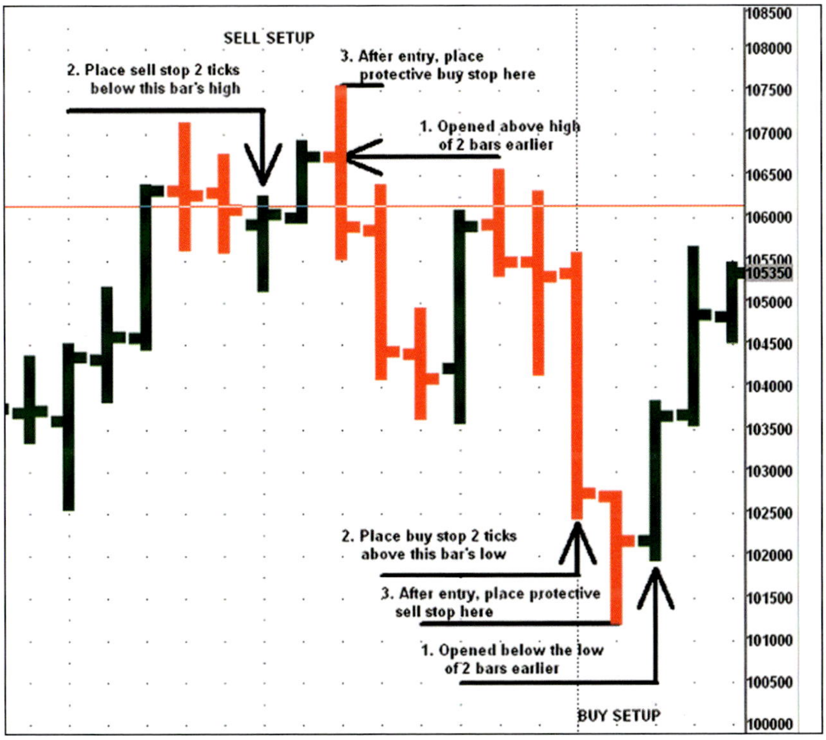

Once the trade is triggered, I put a protective buy stop two ticks above the high of the current bar. If the market trades at or above that high, the protective stop will be triggered. Using this method is an easy way to assess the risk parameters and decide whether the trade makes sense from a risk/reward standpoint.

The lower portion of the chart shows a buy setup. If a market opens below the low of two bars earlier (the bar before last), a buy stop should be placed two ticks above that bar's low.

In Chart 3, the trade would be entered on the fifth bar from the right. As you see, that bar opened below the low of two bars earlier and then traded up through that low to trigger a buy signal. For risk control, you could place a protective sell stop two ticks below the low of the entry bar. A trade at or below that price would trigger a stop to take you out of the market. After each bar is completed, you could reduce your risk or lock in some profit by moving the protective stop up just below the newly completed bar.

Chart 3

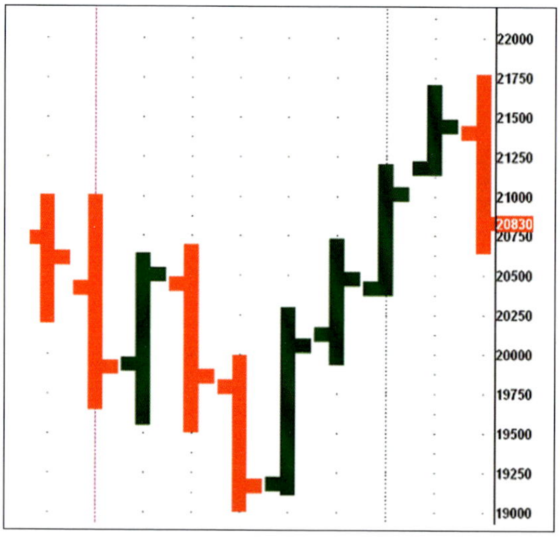

© 2009 eSignal. A division of Interactive Data Corporation (NYSE: IDC).

The protective stop recommended is meant to give you an initial indication of the expected risk. As the trade moves into profit, it makes sense to move the stop along with it to reduce the risk and protect the profit. I usually wait until there is favorable movement before adjusting the stop. Remember that stops become market orders once the stop price is touched, so it is impossible to guarantee an exact amount of risk. Usually the stop is filled on the exact price chosen—give or take one or two ticks.

Finally, in chart 3, notice that a Two-Day Crunch sell signal was given on the last bar of the chart.

Triple Jump

Another effective trend identifier is the Triple Jump. This method uses the extreme price of the past three bars to measure a change in trend. My version of that follows:

To identify the uptrend parameter, we start by finding the highest closing price in a series of higher closes. Count that bar and the two bars immediately preceding it to find the lowest bar range low. That low will become the uptrend parameter. If the market price trades below that bar's low, one could assume that the trend has turned down.

As long as the market stays above that low, the trend is considered to be up. Recalculate if a new high close appears.

For a down trend, find the bar with the lowest closing price and count that bar as well as the two bars immediately preceding it. Use the highest high for that three-bar period as the down-trend parameter. A trade above the high of that bar would indicate a change in the trend from down to up.

As long as the market stays at or below that high, the trend is considered to be down. The trend parameter (the price that would change the trend) will adjust lower as new lower closes are made.

Chart 4
Triple Jumps

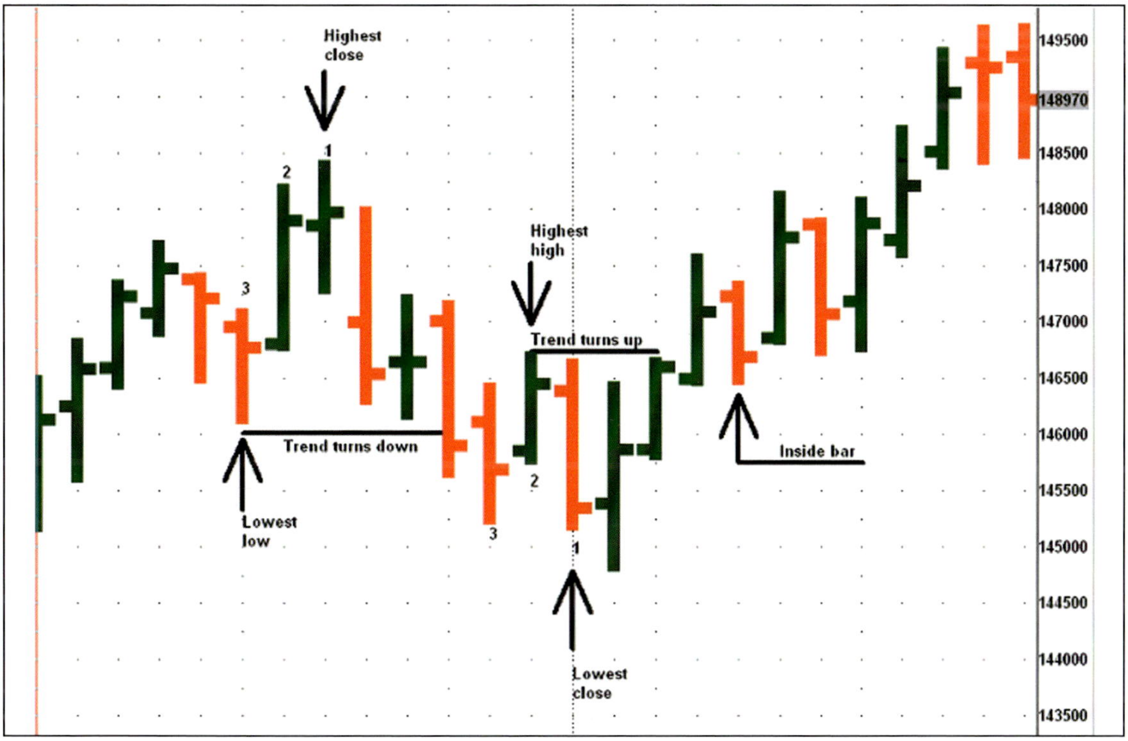

If any of the bars you are counting is an inside bar, drop it and count the preceding bar instead. An inside bar is a bar that has a lower high and a higher low than the bar immediately preceding it

Finally, if an inside bar produces a new high close or a new low close, you would begin the three-bar count with the first normal bar preceding the inside bar.

Failed Reversals

This is another process that has an impressive level of accuracy when you trade in the direction of the existing trend. There is an early hint attached to this that can sometimes provide a much richer opportunity or a tighter risk control for the alert trader.

An upside reversal occurs when a market trades below the previous bar's low and then closes above the previous bar's close.

A downside reversal occurs when the market trades above the high of the previous bar and then closes below the close of the previous bar.

These two occurrences are usually viewed as an indication that the market has changed its mind and will begin to trend in the opposite direction. A failure occurs if the market fails to stay above the low of the up reversal bar or below the high of the down reversal bar. This can result in large volatile market movement. See Chart 6 for examples.

The Hint

There is an early hint that a failure will occur when the market moves below the low of the bar preceding an upside reversal or if the market moves above the high of the bar preceding a downside reversal. That failure signal is a warning that the reversal may be a dud and can sometimes be turned into an excellent trade going in the opposite direction.

In Chart 5, the reversal was the third bar from the left, and the hint was given by the fourth bar when it traded below the low of the second bar. The fourth bar didn't look all that bad, but the hint that there was a problem showed up in a big way in the fifth bar.

Chart 5
The Hint

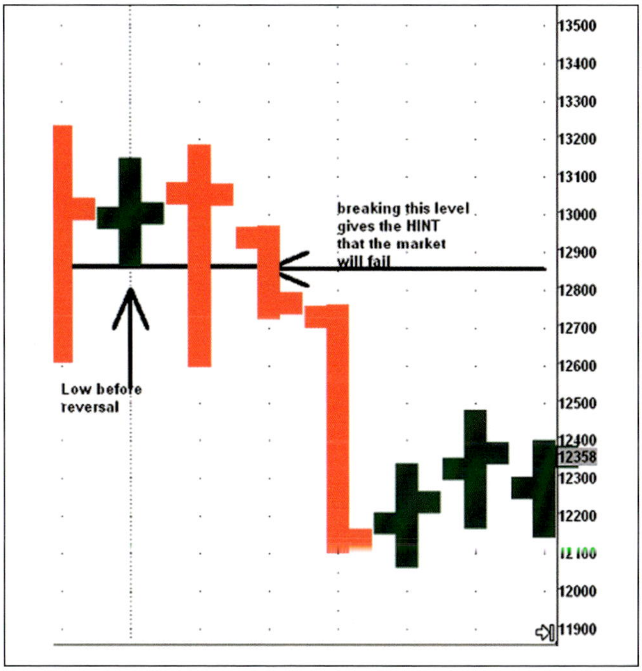

The Hiccup Trigger

This is one of the easiest signals to spot and to use. It works great for short-term trading as well as position accumulation on longer term opportunities.

It really comes in handy if you need to join a fast-moving market in the direction of the trend.

If the market begins to trend and along the way has a small range bar with a counter-trend close, you simply use a stop to enter the market as soon as it resumes the trend.

The key is to enter the market opposite the close of a very small trend bar (Chart 6).

Wrapping It Up

Chart 6 is a gold chart that shows examples of all of the things we've discussed in this chapter. I am not going to waste your time discussing some exotic signal you may never see in your lifetime. As you study this chart, you will find there are signals that weren't labeled. That's good. It means there were even more opportunities in this short span than we have identified. I hope, too, that you notice that not every signal resulted in a big win, although I believe each one did give you a chance to win something.

The hints were able to move you in and out of the market at better prices than some other forms of entry or exit would have.

Chart 6

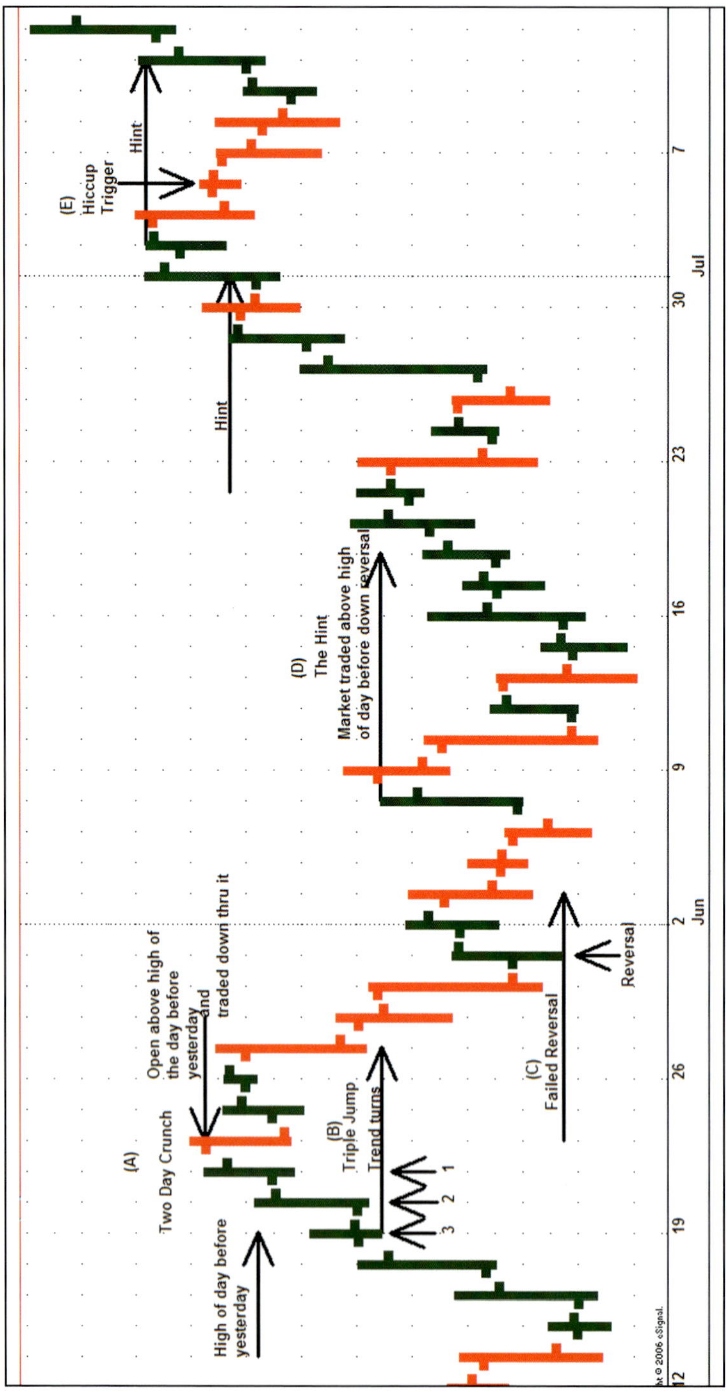

Explanations for Chart 6

A. The Two-Day Crunch. Notice that for three bars after the reversal at the top (bar 8) the market tried and was not able to trade above the high of the bar preceding the reversal (bar 7). That presented a low-risk opportunity to enter the trade with a stop above the hint (the high of bar 7).

B. The Triple Jump. There are four Triple Jumps on this chart. A fifth was narrowly averted at the extreme of the hiccup trade.

C. The Failed Reversal. Notice that the market held for two bars above the low of the bar preceding the reversal before it finally failed. You can see that two bars before the reversal failure there was a Two-Day Crunch sell signal that would have paid nicely.

D. The Hint. I identified only three of the six potential hints on this chart. All reversals will have a hint. The hint at D had a delayed response while the next two were immediate results.

E. The Hiccup Trigger. There were only three of these on this chart, and they were all borderline triggers. The good thing with these is that you have small risk parameters to begin with and can immediately begin to bring protective stops in behind the trade. The big winner here was a couple of days after the Two-Day Crunch.

8
Swing Trading

Swing trading combines trend trading, market timing, money management, and simplicity to create solid results.

Trading with the trend is the best practice, and timing the entry always makes good sense. Using protective stops is an important money-management tool, as is setting a profit target.

There are two basic approaches to almost any kind of trading. One is long-term trend trading, which I would compare to hitting a home run in baseball—very gratifying but hard to do. The other is shorter term trading, which would be more like a base hit—also gratifying and much easier to accomplish. Swing trading fits the second category.

Most of us are a little too impatient to be long-term traders. There's nothing wrong with that as long as we recognize our tendencies and find a plan that fits us naturally. My preference is to choose higher short-term probability over lower long-term possibility. That's not to say that long-term trade projections have less probability than short term. The difference comes in the trader's degree of willingness to stay in a trade for an extended period of time. For many of us, hanging in there takes more energy and discipline than we care to exercise.

Short-term trading usually means less risk and less profit potential. The cost of doing business pretty much stays the same. That means that the short-term trader needs to be working with a higher probability of success than the long-term trader. That's where swing trading comes in.

Basically, my version of swing trading works like this: Identify markets that are already in a trend or have attained a goal and have clearly reversed and begun a new trend; then wait for a correction to develop (counter trend). Once that has occurred, take a measurement that will give a high probability target. You should also measure for other targets with more potential profit even though they may be less likely to be hit. My preference is to take profit at the first target because it should have a significantly higher probability of being reached.

Protective stops are established as soon as a trade is entered, but the amount of risk is not determined until then because the market action preceding entry often determines the stop placement. You should move your stops into a low, no risk, or profitable situation as soon as it makes sense to do so.

As an example, if you enter a market and it quickly moves to within easy reach of your first target, you should move your stop to the point of entry to reduce exposure on a trade that almost made it. Sometimes it makes sense to take profit early if you're close to the target and the market is about to close for the day. These are money management decisions that can increase the winning probabilities and often the bottom line.

Swing trading offers opportunity for accounts of almost every size. Larger accounts can participate in all of the trade opportunities and increase the number of contracts traded to suit their appetites. Medium accounts can trade one or two contracts and be a little more selective about the size of the market being traded. Small accounts can trade single contracts in less volatile markets.

Tools for the Trade

Basic bar charts will work just fine. I like to include Bollinger Bands in almost all of my trading strategies. The middle line on the Bollinger Bands is the 20 Bar Average—one of my favorites. I also use the 8 Bar Average and the 5 Bar Average to help me qualify trades. Occasionally, a 3 Bar Exponential Average can be used as well. Beyond that, you need to be able to calculate percentages and add.

At one time, probably fifteen to twenty years ago, I happened to measure the last move in a market before it hit its low and started to trade back up. The nature of markets is for them to occasionally correct themselves no matter how strong or weak they are. My hope was to be able to project the size of those corrections by relating them to the distance most recently traveled. That market actually traveled back up farther than it had come down. In a few days it became apparent that it had turned the trend upward.

I did a quick measurement and found that the market had rallied exactly twice the distance of the final down move. That seemed interesting enough and motivated me to check out dozens of instances where the same combination of events occurred. In the process it became apparent that more often than not the market failed to double itself back—at least not right away.

It's fun for me to share ideas with the people who trade with me and are willing to listen, so I did that in this case. I showed a good friend of mine in Colorado what I had found, and we agreed that we had something that could be valuable. However, since it usually took a long time for our double back scenario to work out, we pretty much forgot about it and went on to other things.

Last summer my Colorado buddy called me all excited and told me he'd discovered something that I wouldn't believe. He said that one evening just for fun he had gone back to our old idea of measuring the market for double-backs and realized that we had failed to notice something else that happened with an amazing amount of reliability.

What he discovered was that, once the market reversed enough to exceed the high of the last move downward or the low of the last move upward, it would continue to move in the direction of the reversal for an additional 60 percent and much of the time for 100 percent.

I was skeptical but told him that I would check it out as time permitted. I did and became just as enthusiastic as he was. Of course, nothing like this works every time, so it is essential to always exercise caution, but it was amazing to see how consistent the market was in proving out his findings.

Let's take a look at how this works through the use of a simple bar chart. Chart 1 (bear market chart) gives some good examples of how this can play out in a market that is declining.

Look for the market to make a move that has some continuity such as three or more lower closes in a row or a move that has a greater range than a similar number of previous bars. Wait for a completed counter trend (in this case an upward rally) and place a sell stop just below the low that preceded the counter trend.

A suggestion for taking profit would be to measure the range of the recent counter trend and find out how many points 60 percent of that range is. Subtract that number of points from the recent low and place an order to buy at that price.

There is nothing magical about 60 percent except that the market frequently reaches that distance early in the trade. I regularly use 60 percent and sometimes, if it looks like the market is in a trend, it makes sense to keep the trade for a while longer and just follow it with stops. There is a good chance it will reach 100 percent and has a reasonable shot at 150 percent.

On Chart 1, the number of ticks representing the size of the rally is written on the "counter trend" lines. These are the numbers that you use to get the 60 percent, 100 percent, and 150 percent target figures.

Notice on Chart 1 how quickly the market hit the first target after the lows preceding the rallies were broken. Each signal on this chart paid out more than 60 percent of the previous rally in two bars or less. The second trade shown on this chart actually hit the 150 percent mark for a healthy profit of approximately $5. Not only that, but all three targets were hit in the first bar!

Chart 1
Bear Market Swings

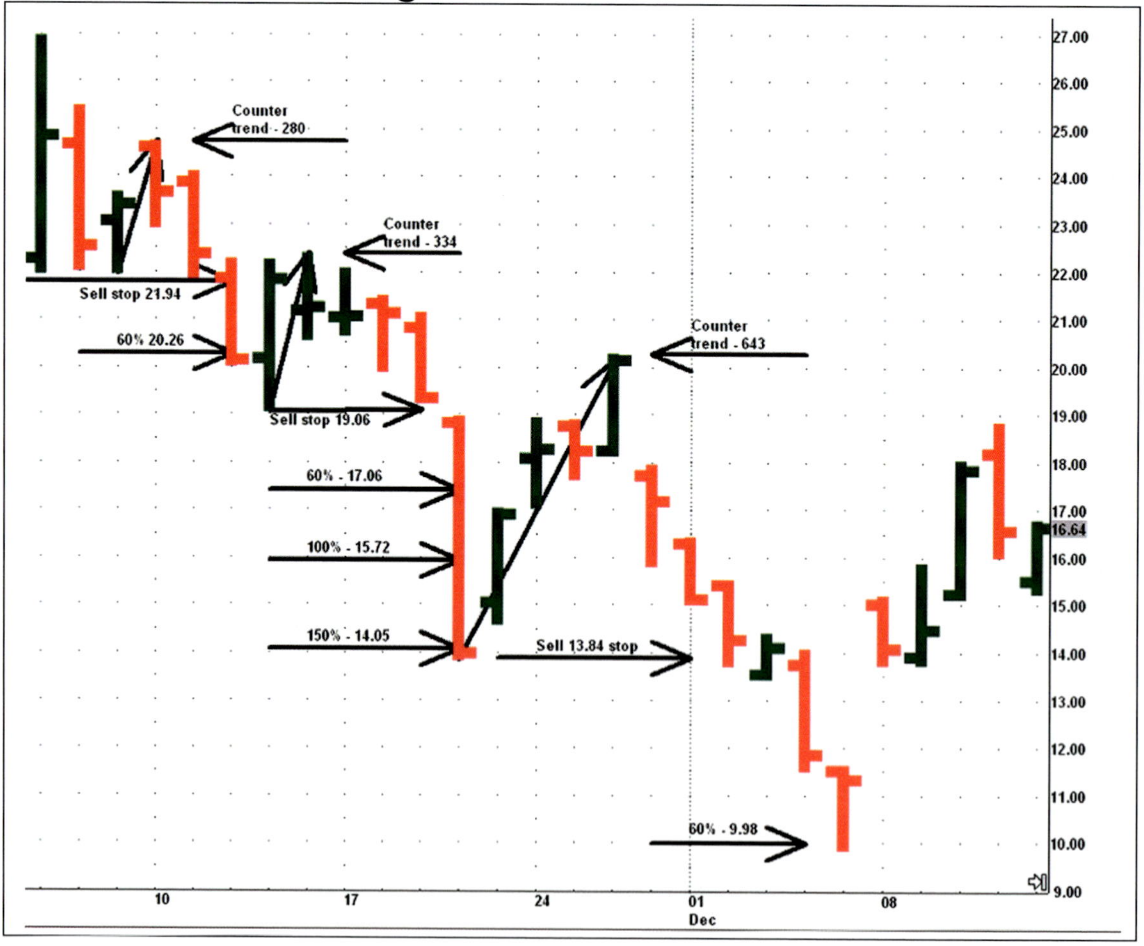

Bull Market Swings

This time you look for a market that has continuity moving upward. Wait for a completed counter trend bar and place a buy stop just above the recent high. On Chart 2, the entry stop points are marked with arrows. Measure the recent pull back, find 60 percent of that range, and add that amount to the recent high. That should establish a likely price to take a short-term profit.

On Chart 2 there were three trades, and each one immediately continued for more than the minimum 60 percent objective.

On Chart 2 you can also see that the fourth and fifth bars from the right represent a rally that failed, setting up a bear market swing (unmarked). When the low of the fifth bar was broken, the 60 percent target was reached almost immediately.

These opportunities present themselves on a regular basis. All you need to do is place the trades and follow the rules.

Chart 2
Bull Market Swings

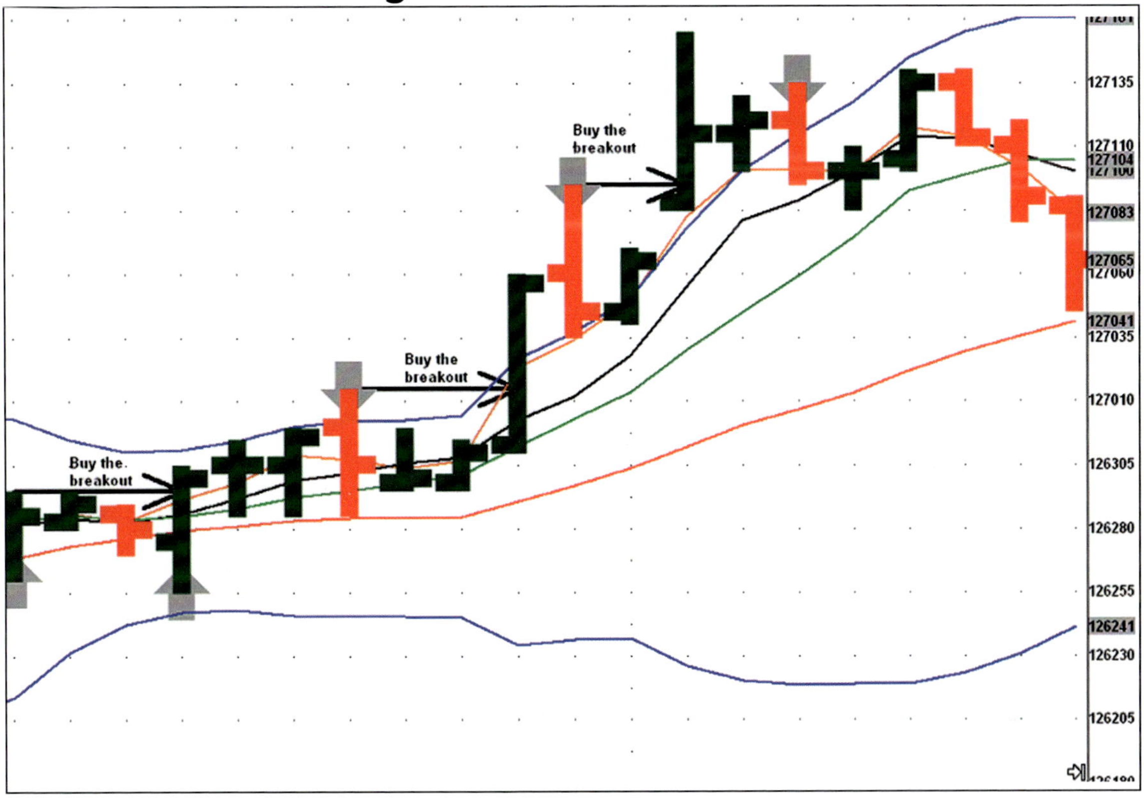

If this is the method you choose to trade, I recommend you use two or three momentum studies that you prefer on your bar charts whenever you trade. Momentum indicators can be extremely useful in helping you choose the right time and place to make a trade.

Not every swing trade will be a winner, but you can certainly sort out the lower probability setups by watching and analyzing the current momentum. I usually carry the 20 Bar Average, 8 Bar Average, and Bollinger Bands on my charts. In Chart 3 the Bollinger Bands (blue lines) use a simple 20 Bar Average as the anchor line or mid point. The 5 (black), 8 (green), and 20 (red) are all simple moving averages with the movement based on the most recent price. Occasionally, the 3 Bar Exponential Moving Average (orange) gets to be a part of the fun. Finally, it is sometimes useful to keep an eye on the stochastics since they can often warn you of an impending change in the direction of the momentum.

These are my favorite momentum indicators, but you may have others that you prefer. If so, go for it! The most important thing is that you have confidence in the tools you plan to use—and that they deserve your confidence. If they don't, you won't trade very long without recognizing it.

Chart 3
Swing Chart with Studies

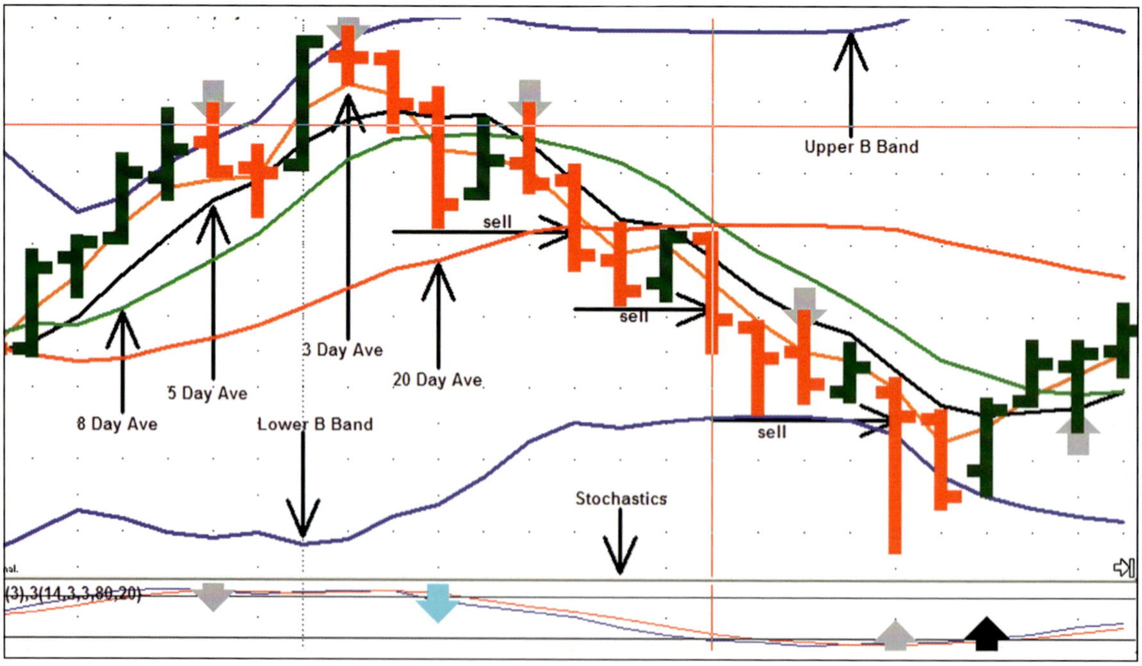

No trade should be made without first assessing the risk involved and its relationship with the anticipated reward. The standard approach to risk/reward is that you should never risk more than half of what you expect to gain. That sounds fine but begs a couple of major questions. First, are you factoring in commissions and slippage when you consider your risk, and are you subtracting them from your expected reward? If not, you might be sorely disappointed in your net results.

The second question has to do with probabilities. Does the same formula apply to high probability trades as it does to low? I have some methods of trading that require a greater risk than others, but it doesn't bother me because the probability of winning is much higher. Every trader must determine what his or her own comfort level is for risk. I typically do not let the market go beyond the other end of the entry bar.

If we short the market and it turns down, it makes sense to put a buy stop above that bar's high, and if the entry was a buy, to put a sell stop below that bar's low. Stops are placed immediately after entry.

Basic Checklist for Swing Trading

1. What is the direction and power of the momentum?
    - Remember that trading against power reduces the probability of success.

2. How and where will I enter the trade?
    - Buy a breakout or sell a breakdown.
    - Enter a priced order on a pull back of 40–60 percent of either a previous bar or continuous market run.

3. How will I control the risk and what will it be?
    - Always use a protective stop.
    - Make the market take out a price level that has been tested earlier and held.
    - On breakouts and breakdowns, risk very little.

4. Do I have more than one target?
    - Always have a probable and a possible trade goal.
    - Put the target in immediately. (Notice Chart 3; the last trade hit 100 percent and came back to where it started in the same bar.)

5. Does the risk/reward ratio work?
    - Make sure the probable goal is at least twice the risk.

6. How will I adjust as the trade progresses?
    - Take a profit when the target is hit.
    - Move the stop to a profit position when it makes sense.
    - When you move the stop, be aware that the market pulls back to the center of previous bars, so don't move into a price area that is almost certain to be visited.

9
Shadow Trading

Many of the strategies that I use are short-term trading plans that often can be parlayed into much larger plays, and with patience and discipline, can firmly set up a long-term trend trade. Shadow trading is just such a plan. My trade plans will always provide you with an entry point, a protective stop, and a realistic profit goal that, in my opinion, should almost always be attained.

In candlestick charting, there is a part of the daily bar that is called the shadow. I am not suggesting or requiring that you use candlestick trading in the method I am about to describe, but we are going to steal the idea of the shadow for our purposes.

The necessary ingredients for shadow trading will include the Bollinger Bands, bar charts or candlestick charts, and an 8 Period Simple Average. In the examples shown in Chart 1 you will see two moving lines between the Bollinger Bands. The slower line (red) represents a 20 Bar Simple Moving Average, and the more active line (green) is the 8 Bar Simple Moving Average.

A bare-bones explanation of the shadow trade is this: If the market has recently touched the Bollinger Band and then penetrated the 8 Bar Average, it frequently will continue on for an additional 60 percent move and often continue directly to the opposite Bollinger Band.

Chart 1

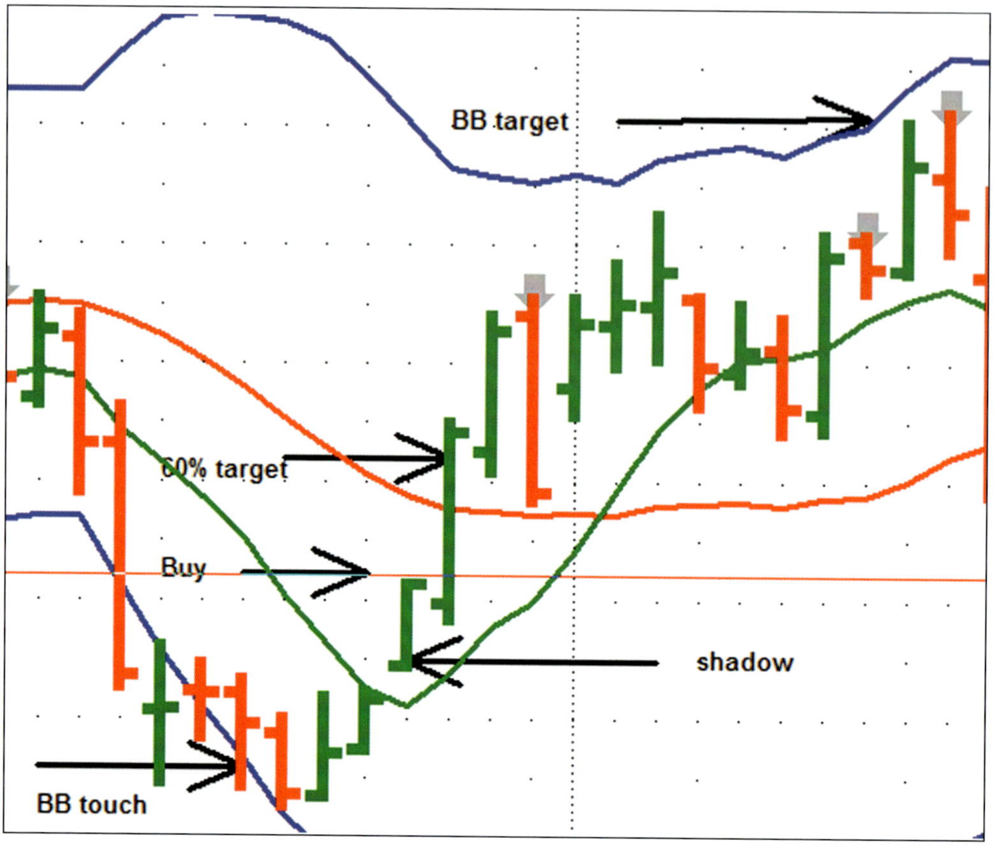

Shadow trading signals will often precede a change in the moving average. I use an 8 Bar Simple Moving Average most of the time and rely on it to identify the trend. Many times the shadow trade requires me to step outside of my box to trade against the trend. I am willing to do that because it is easy to establish a risk/reward ratio before committing to the trade.

When I first started to trade the shadows, it was so hard for me to break my commitment to the 8 Bar Average that I added a 3 Bar Exponential Average and a 5 Bar Simple Average to my charts for encouragement. They are both extremely useful in the process of verifying the quality of the potential trade.

Let's say that a market has been falling for several periods and has reached or exceeded the lower Bollinger Band. You can expect the 8 and 20 Period Moving Averages to be tagging along.

After the lower Bollinger Band has been touched, the market might begin to strengthen a bit. This could be a normal correction in a down market, or it could be an opportunity to make some profit.

Any time that a bar penetrates the 8 Period Average line following a touch of the Bollinger Band, a trigger point has been established. The market has left a "shadow" over the moving average line. The casting of the shadow is not the signal. The signal is given when the market subsequently exceeds the high of the shadow bar for a buy. For a sell, the market would have touched the upper Bollinger Band and then penetrated the 8 Period Average line. A drop below the low of that penetration bar would be the signal to sell.

An exception would be if the 3 Bar Exponential Average turns back in the direction of the shadow (see example in Chart 3). In that case, try to enter the market in the middle of the bar that created the shadow and risk the remaining portion of that bar plus one tick.

Will every shadow setup result in a win? Of course not! What it will do is provide you with an opportunity to make a trade that should give you a larger potential profit than the estimated probable risk. Trading is all about possibilities and probabilities. Any time you can find a method that gives you a reasonable opportunity to compare the two, you have an edge over the average trader.

It is a good idea at this time to take a look at the stochastic lines. Chart 2 displays them at the bottom. When the fast "K" line has been below the 20 percent line and is crossing over it to go up, the odds for a win should improve. If you are beginning to think that there are too many restrictions here to ever let a trade filter through, relax. When a trading opportunity is ripe, these indicators have a way of coming together and helping you with the timing and confidence you will need to carry the trade.

Now it is time to set up the trade. Chart 2 will have two examples of buy signals and two examples of sell signals. The first shadow is a sell, the second is a buy, the third is a buy, and the fourth is a sell. You would begin a buy signal by entering a buy stop only one or two ticks above the high of the shadow. If that stop price is hit, it will become a market order and you will buy the market.

Once you are in the market, you need to take care of two things. First, you need to place a protective sell stop just below the low of the shadow period. Second, you need to set a priced sell order above the market as a profit target.

Naturally, for a sell shadow you would enter a sell stop only one or two ticks below the low of the shadow. If that stop price is hit, it will become a market order, and you will be short in the market. As soon as that happens, you will need to place a protective buy stop just above the high of the shadow period and then set a priced buy order in below the market at your profit target.

Chart 2

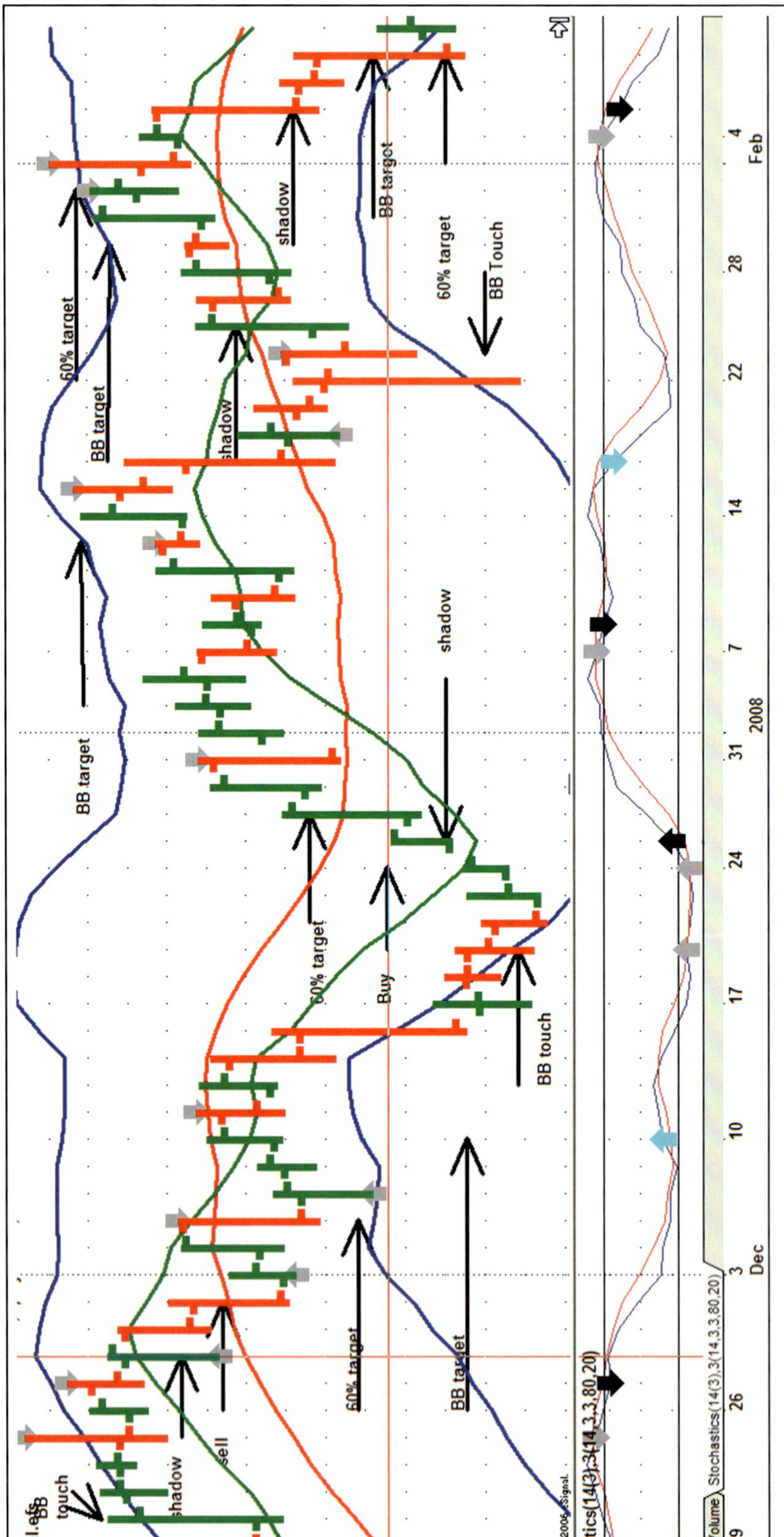
BB target
60% target
shadow
Buy
sell
BB touch
BB Touch
Stochastics(14(3),3(14,3,3,80,20)
Volume
19
26
3
Dec
10
17
24
31
2008
7
14
22
28
4
Feb

The amount of profit to go for is strictly a personal choice, but I have found that there are goals that most markets attain with an amazing degree of probability.

Setting targets will give you an edge.

My favorite method for setting a target in shadow trading for a buy signal is to use the upper Bollinger Band price as it existed at the time of the shadow bar and place an order to sell at that price.

Conversely, you would use the lower Bollinger Band as it existed at the time of the shadow bar to take profit on a short sell. The target needs to remain the same even though the Bollinger Band probably will move several times before the goal is attained.

Another one of my favorites is the 60 percent target. To determine the price for the target in a market that has given a shadow buy signal, we would measure the distance in points from the high of the shadow to the recent significant low. In this case, you would then add 60 percent of that range to the high of the shadow to find your target price.

For a shadow sell signal, the measuring would be the same, but you would subtract the 60 percent from the low of the shadow bar.

Using those two methods gives you two targets to aim for and the choice to accept less profit with higher probability or possibly greater gains with the more extreme number. When going for the more distant target, be sure to bring your protective stop into a profitable position so that, if the market fails to make the second goal, there will still be a payday.

The markets are random but do have repetitive tendencies. It is important to understand that the targets are not always met. Our goal here is to set up a plan that will give you an edge in these random markets. It is highly unlikely that a random act in a random market will outperform a plan based on repetitive patterns. Sharpshooters typically don't shoot from the hip and neither should we.

Chart 3 shows a situation where the Bollinger Band target was closer than the 60 percent target. In this case you might have preferred to take the closer target, but if not, it would have been important to at least protect some of your profit (perhaps a two-bar crunch buy stop) while you shoot for the bigger goal. As you can see, the larger goal was not attained.

Chart 3

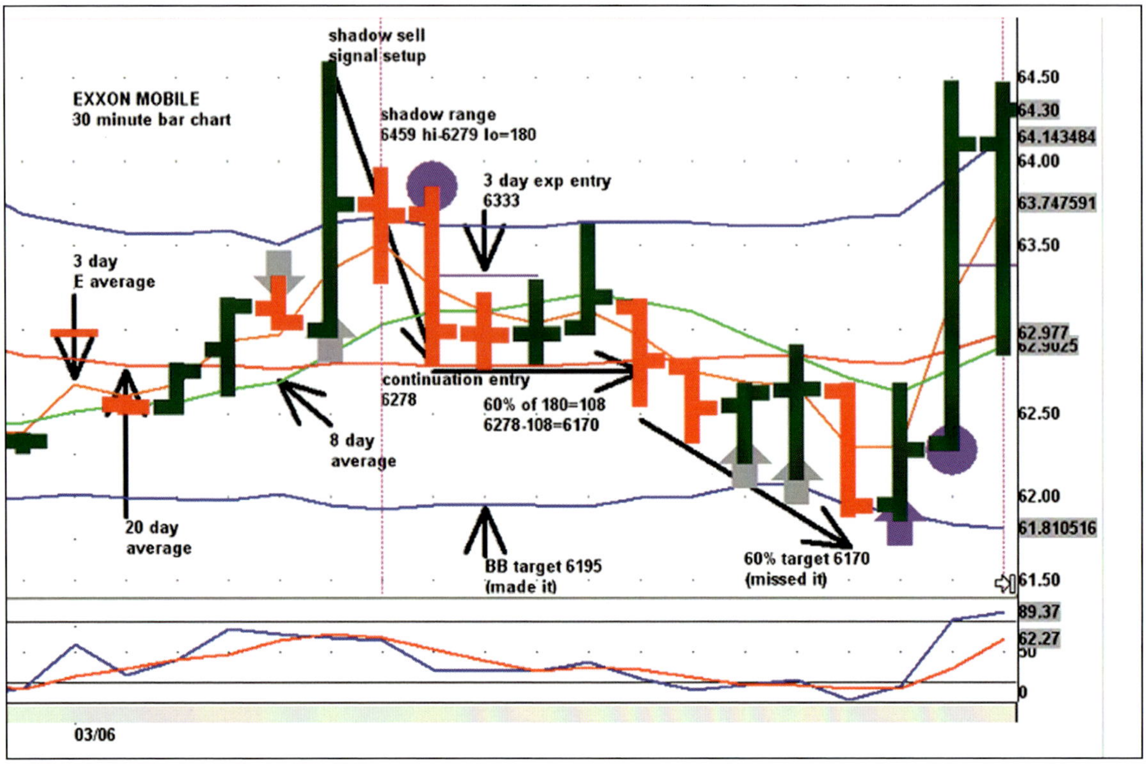

Sometimes the shadow signal can be used to help you find a good protective stop point for a longer term trade that you already have on. Chart 4 shows how we used it to exit a long position. We were in a profitable position that had potential for more profit but wanted to be out if there was the likelihood of a deep correction. As you can see, the method served us well. Measurement indicated a minimum move down to 9880 with the second target at 9125. The shadow trigger was 10740. The targets were both well below the original point of entry, so it made sense to step aside when the trigger was tripped.

Chart 4

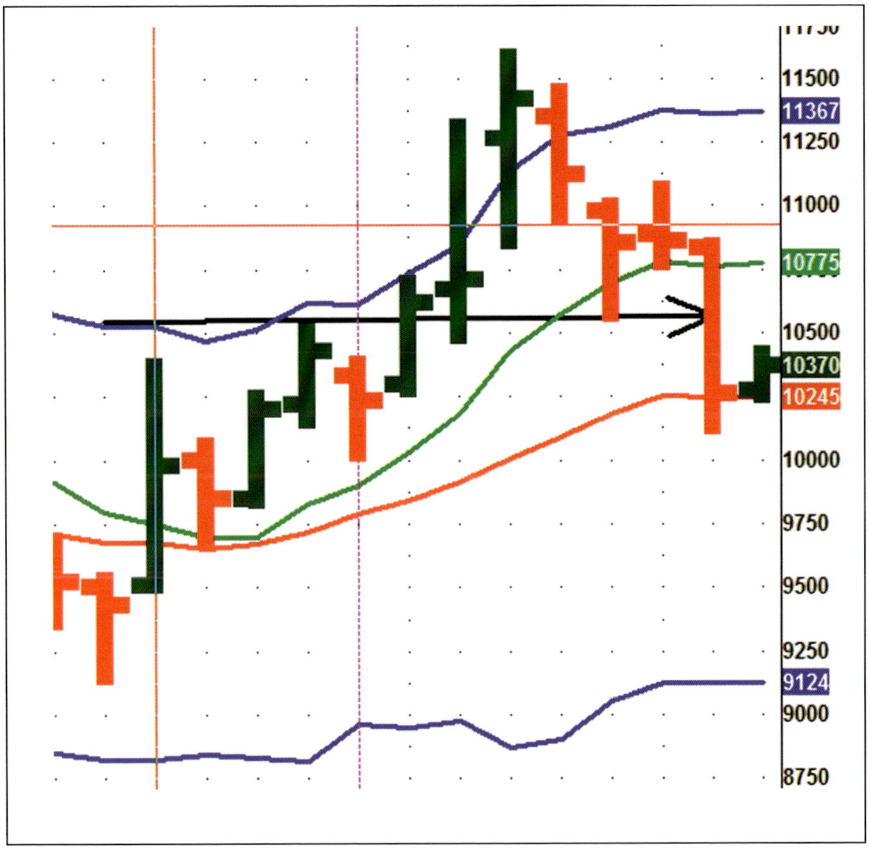

Once spotting shadows becomes easy for you to do quickly, you will find yourself sorting out which trades to take based on the risk/reward ratio being offered.

For instance, if you have a target that will make you 60 points but the protective stop is being carried 120 points away, you might pass on that trade because you are risking twice as much as you hope to make. Of course, you have the options of going for more profit (maybe 100 percent) or moving the stop closer, which can usually be done as soon as you move into a new period. You might also decide that the probability of the trade being a winner is so high that the larger risk is justified.

My personal preference when I enter the market with a stop order is to closely guard my position with a protective stop. This is one kind of entry that justifies impatience. The reason is that entering with a stop is usually done because we expect the market to take off and run away. If we didn't expect that to happen, we would be better off waiting patiently for a pull back after the market has given the signal.

Trades happen both ways, so there is no right answer. Remember this: If you buy a breakout, put your stop in tight, and then get knocked out, it doesn't mean that the signal was wrong. You can still put an order in to enter the market in the direction of the original signal, perhaps at a better price level.

Remember that you can use the Bollinger Band in front of the market as one of your targets. The market will frequently reach the target Bollinger Band value that was existent at the close of the shadow period.

The 60 percent extension is my favorite target in most cases, but be aware that if the 20 Period Average is between the shadow and the target, it could be a point of resistance.

It has been said that greed and fear can be the trader's worst enemies or best friends. I suggest that you try to always find a balance between them if you intend to trade successfully.

Check List for Shadow Trading

1. What is the direction and power of the momentum?
    - Remember that trading against power reduces the probability of success.
    - Usually the momentum will be less aggressive at the time a shadow trade occurs.
    - If the 8 Bar Average is moving in the opposite direction sharply at the time of the shadow signal, it might be best to enter the market on a retracement rather than a breakout. Remember that you should wait to trade until the odds are favorable.

2. How and where will I enter the trade?
    - Buy a breakout or sell a breakdown using a stop order.
    - Enter on a pull back of 40–60 percent of either a previous bar or continuous market run.
    - Once again, be cautious about going against an 8 Bar Average if it is moving counter to your trade direction with a steep angle.

3. How will I control the risk and what will it be?
    - Always use a protective stop.
    - Make the market take out a price level that has been tested earlier and held.
    - On breakouts and breakdowns, risk very little.

4. Do I have more than one target?
  - Always have a probable and a possible trade goal.

5. Does the risk/reward ratio work?
  - Make sure the probable goal is at least twice the risk.

6. How will I adjust as the trade progresses?
  - Take a profit when the target is hit.
  - Move the stop to a profit position when it makes sense.
  - If you are trying for a second target, be sure to protect the first target profit as soon as possible.

10

Breakouts and Band Running

Joining markets that are on the run is always a dangerous but exciting way to trade. I must admit that it isn't the type of trading I prefer, although I find myself doing it quite often. I know that it can be quite rewarding but also extremely destructive.

If you feel the need to jump into a high-momentum market situation, let me suggest a few things that could help you come away with some success.

No one I know of can guarantee a market prediction's result, so all we can really do is put together some suggestions that could help us gain an edge in moving with the market effectively. It is easy to be caught up in the excitement of a runaway market, so it is most important for you to get a grip on your emotions and do your best to avoid making quick, regrettable decisions. Don't forget that your reason for trading is to show a profit—not just to make a trade.

Some might say that we are chasing the market with this type of trading, and to many that would be a "no-no." I would prefer to say that we have waited to join the market until we are convinced that it is more likely to continue its next surge.

CATCHING A RUNAWAY MARKET TAKES NERVE

It is important in every trade, but especially this type, to do an emotional checkup on yourself before you pull the trigger. If you are afraid of the trade before you enter, it is highly likely you will be unable to hold on for a profit. It is much better to be honest with yourself and pass on the trade than it is to jump in and then bail out with a loss for reasons that are purely emotional.

For instance, a lot of traders like to buy breakouts. That is a situation where a market suddenly moves into a higher level than it has been for some time. These trades can be excellent opportunities because of the excitement they generate on their own as well as the possible fundamental forces that might be driving the market, but they also often require that you enter far away from any realistic protective stop point.

My main approach to this problem is based in the reasoning that convinced me to buy the market in this manner in the first place. If I think this market is so dynamic that I won't get an opportunity to buy it at a better price in the near future—or maybe ever—then it seems reasonable to expect it to take off and go without delay. In my mind there is no room for any pull back at that point.

For instance, if you are buying a breakout, plan to find a protective stop point either below the low of the period that broke the market out or sometimes even below the most recent five-minute period. Do not allow it to go below the low of the last pull back or close below the close of the entry bar without making an exit.

Another excellent protective stop point with this type of trade is to carry a sell stop in an up market just below the high of two bars earlier, provided the market opens above that high (Chart 1a).

In a down market, you would carry a protective buy stop just above the low of two bars earlier, provided the market opened below the low of that bar.

Remember that there will be an infinite number of trading opportunities but for most of us a limited amount of capital. Preserve the capital!

Notice how the breakout level is well above any short-term support in Chart 1a. The first close was soft, but the market continued in spite of that.

Chart 1a

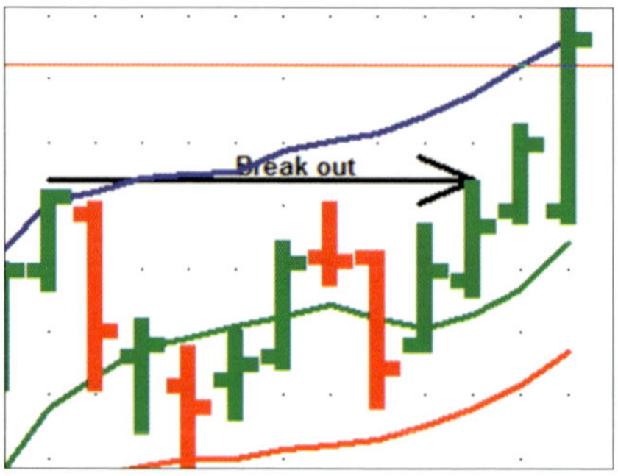

Chart 1b represents a failed signal. Notice how the breakout period itself was unable to close strong and was followed by more weakness right away. Notice also that the bar after the breakout bar opened above the high of the second previous bar. A stop right below the high of that bar would have reduced the risk significantly.

Chart 1b

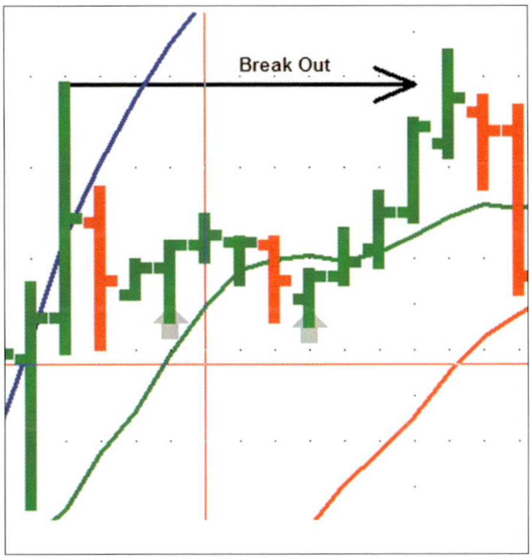

In both examples, the breakout period did not produce a close that would create much excitement. There is a tendency for many of us to want to abandon the trade simply because it didn't behave perfectly on the first period. Having a workable method for entry is a wonderful thing but pretty much useless if we aren't patient enough to wait for our trade to prove itself.

In Chart 1a, the breakout proved to be an excellent trade. In Chart 1b, it failed and lost money. The challenge is to understand that we are dealing with a level of randomness that will sometimes cause us to lose money no matter how smart we are or how reliable our methods are.

If we had taken both of these trades, used the suggested risk management and been patient with them, we would have achieved a successful outcome over a three-bar period in spite of the one trade that failed.

Band Running

For this type of trading, it is necessary to have the Bollinger Bands and a 5 Period Simple Moving Average on your chart. In the setup that you will be looking for, the closing price of the most recent period will be above the upper Bollinger Band for a buy long or below the lower band for a sell short. Along with that, it is essential that the relevant Bollinger Band is moving in the direction of the market at a steep angle and also that the 5 Period Simple Average is keeping pace with or catching up with the Bollinger Band (Chart 2a).

This is what a buy long Bollinger Band Runner would look like.

Chart 2a

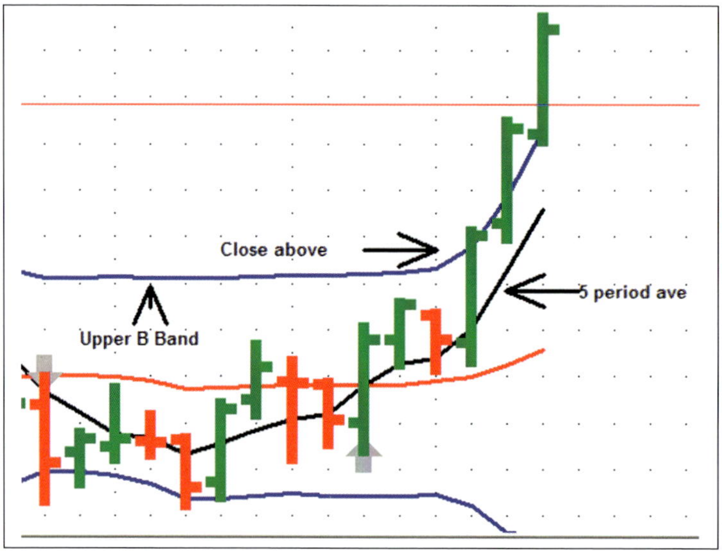

© 2009 eSignal. A division of Interactive Data Corporation (NYSE: IDC).

This is what a sell short Bollinger Band Runner would look like.

Chart 2b

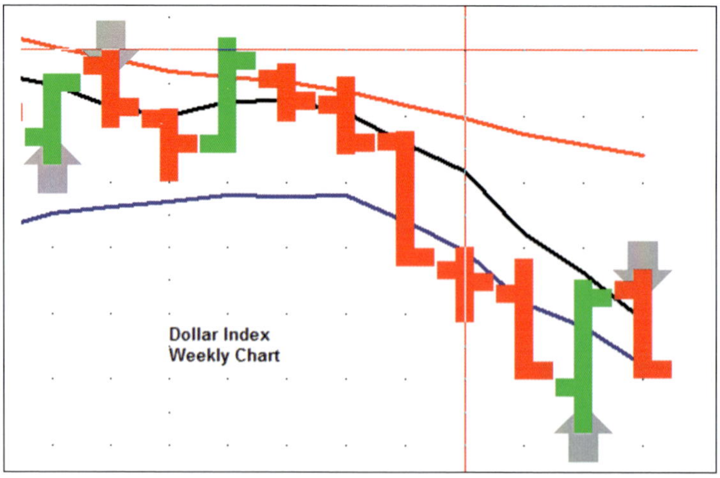

© 2009 eSignal. A division of Interactive Data Corporation (NYSE: IDC).

Notice that in both charts the closes broke outside of the Bollinger Band and continued for three periods. That is a fairly typical occurrence. Also notice in chart 2b, where the closes were below the Band, that even though the market then closed above the Band on the fourth period, the 5 Bar Moving Average continued to move closer to the lower Band, which would indicate that the existing downward momentum is still intact. Remember—the Bollinger Band needs to be moving at a fairly sharp angle.

Risk Control

Risk control is essential in this kind of trading. My chosen method is to immediately place a sell stop just below the low of the range of an upward breakout period. After the second period, move the stop up to just below the second period's low. On the third period, leave it there and from then on carry the stop below the lowest low of the two most recent periods. Some might want to keep the stop just below the low of the most recently completed period.

The process would be reversed for a breakout to the downside. After the first close below the Bollinger Band, I would place a buy stop just above the high of that period. After the second period, I would move the stop down to just above the high of the second period. It would stay at the same place for the third period, and from then on it would always stay just above the highest high for the two most recent periods.

It might be just as profitable, or even more so, to keep the stop just above the high of the most recently completed period.

Don't forget about the two-day crunch stop for trades going either direction.

A warning: There is sometimes a temptation to bring the protective stop inside the range of the current period. Many times that is a shortcut to lower profits. When traders ask me if they should bring their stop in really close, I usually tell them they might as well just get out. Most of the time the market will take them out anyway, and getting out right where they are will save them money.

The exception to this is when a target has been reached and the trader wants to give the market a chance to continue on without giving up a lot of profit. In those situations it makes sense to use a fifteen-, thirty-, or sixty-minute chart to help find the best placement for a tight protective stop.

Exiting the Trade

There are as many opinions on how to exit a trade as there are ways to do it, but the one thing that seems to signal the end most reliably is a widening of the gap between the 5 Period Average and the outside Bollinger Band. As soon as you see a widening begin to happen, it is probably time to leave the scene.

Some traders want to let the market decide, so they either continue with their protective stop plan or accelerate it.

Sometimes you might just close out your position at the market as soon as you see the signals of a slower momentum.

Remember your reason for being in this trade in the first place. You wanted to take advantage of a running market. As soon as the reason for being there begins to fade, either exit or protect. There are so many great trading opportunities available that there is little justification for staying with one once it gets stale.

Study Chart 3 and observe how the black line (5 Bar Average) is closing the gap with the blue (Bollinger Band) line and then begins to separate even though the market itself continued to decline.

Remember to trust your plan. Even a good plan will sometimes fail, but the discipline of a good plan will give you a real edge.

Chart 3

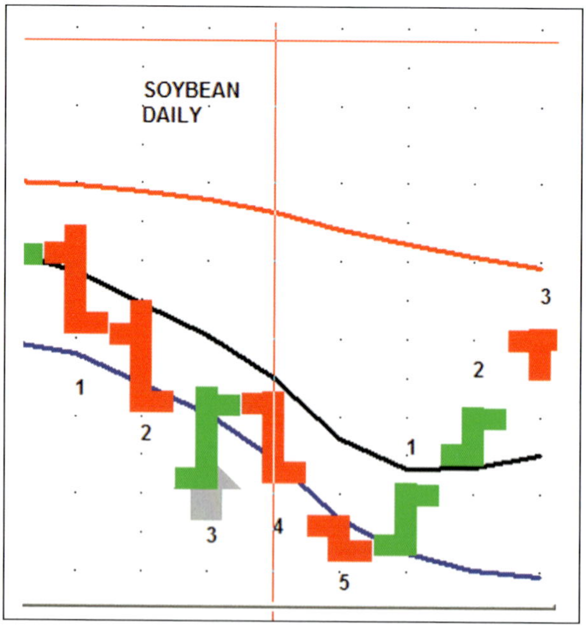

© 2009 eSignal. A division of Interactive Data Corporation (NYSE: IDC).

Notice the distance between the Bollinger Band and the 5 Bar Average begins to widen at the low (5) bar and then becomes more pronounced on the following (1) bar. One should probably exit at the close of the 5 bar and certainly when the high of the 5 bar is breached.

Chart 4 has a 3 Bar Exponential Average (orange) added to the mix just to show how much quicker it is to show weakness in the momentum. Using the 3 Bar Average could be an advantage, but it could also take you out of the market too early. The green line is an 8 Bar Simple Moving Average.

Chart 4

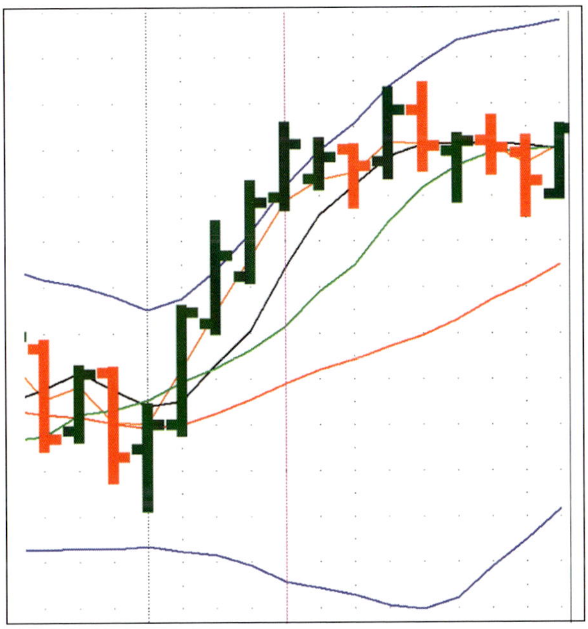

Every trade you make should have a general structure.

There should be:

1. A plan for entering
2. A plan for controlling risk
3. A plan for staying with the trade
4. A plan that deals with your expectations
5. A plan to exit

Be sure that your checklist deals with all five of these areas.

If a trader fails to form or implement the plan at any of these levels, the probability of success will be severely limited. Remember that these methods are simply suggested tools to help increase the edge that you could have in trading. Success must come from the trader and his or her willingness and discipline to use the tools.

11

One-Day Wonders

Now that we have looked at market formations, it's time to check out the wealth of valuable information contained in a single bar. I call these "one-day wonders," but the qualities we'll discuss will apply to single bars for any time duration—even one-minute bars.

For the sake of simplicity let's assume each bar represents one day although these tactics can be applied to both shorter and longer term bars.

Remember that the opening price of a bar represents a value assigned by the trading community at the beginning of the bar. The close represents the consensus at period's end, and the range represents the emotional highs and lows that occurred between those times.

The high records the price level where the sellers began to outnumber the buyers. The low shows the point where the buyers finally outnumbered the sellers for that particular bar.

Markets are an auction.

These markets are really a large continuous auction where you can bid on something you want to buy, hold it for a while, and then put it back into the auction for sale just like a vendor would. Of course, at a typical auction you don't normally resell the item you bought on the same day. Usually it has to be paid for and you would bring it back at a later date for sale. In the market, you take immediate ownership of a product and can then dispose of it as soon as you like. Knowing the components of the previous bar can be a great help in a situation like that.

There are three types of bar ranges that I like best to work with technically. They are reversal bars, outside bars, and large-range bars.

Large-range bars are more subjective than the others because you need to define large. There is no absolute here, but I deal with this issue by visually comparing those bars to what would appear to be an average range for the market being traded.

Outside bars are periods that have exceeded both the high and the low of the previous bar.

Reversal bars are periods when the market has either gone higher than the previous bar's high and then closed below the previous close or gone lower than the bar before and closed above the previous close.

One of the things that all three of these types have in common is that, within a short time (usually the next bar), the market will move back to or a little bit through the middle of the original bar's range.

Remember this! It will prove to be very valuable information! The following charts will give examples of this for each type.

On Chart 1 you can see that, following the first large-range bar, the market came back up to the middle and then started to go back down. On the very next bar the target was hit. Here is the play-by-play:

- Large-range bar – High 1453, Low 1379—Range 74 points.
- Middle of range – 1416 (This is the point of entry to go short.)
- Target—74 × .60 = 44 points
- Subtract 44 from the Low (1379)—1379 - 44 = 1335 (price target)
- Potential—1416 (entry point) - 1335 (target price) = 81 points
- Risk—Buy stop at 1454 (High of first large range) 1454 - 1416 = 38 points

The high of the entry bar was 1453, so there was plenty of room to make the entry. The low of the exit bar was 1297, which also allowed plenty of room to close the trade out. The risk price represents the original risk that can be reduced or eliminated as the market moves in your favor.

Notice that shortly after the target was reached, the market traveled back up to the middle of the most recent large-range bar to begin the second successful trade.

There are two really valuable behaviors associated with reversal, outside, and large-range bars. The first is that the market returns to the center of those bars with a high degree of reliability. Simply knowing that one thing should give the trader an edge. It could be played for the return or could be used to improve the quality of the entry. It could reduce the risk and increase the profit potential of the trade by a significant amount just for starters.

The second characteristic related to these bars is that no matter which end of the bar's range the market decides to violate, it will often continue beyond that point of violation for at least another 60 percent. The probabilities of this happening are better if the continuation is in the direction of the existing trend, but either way the odds are still very good.

Do the math. If the previous bar has a 100 point range and you enter the market later when it breaks out of that range, you can expect the market to go another 60 points or more. Not bad! Better yet, if you join the market at the middle of the 100 point bar and it breaks out in your direction, you have the opportunity to make 110 points. Even better!!

Chart 1
Large-Range Bar

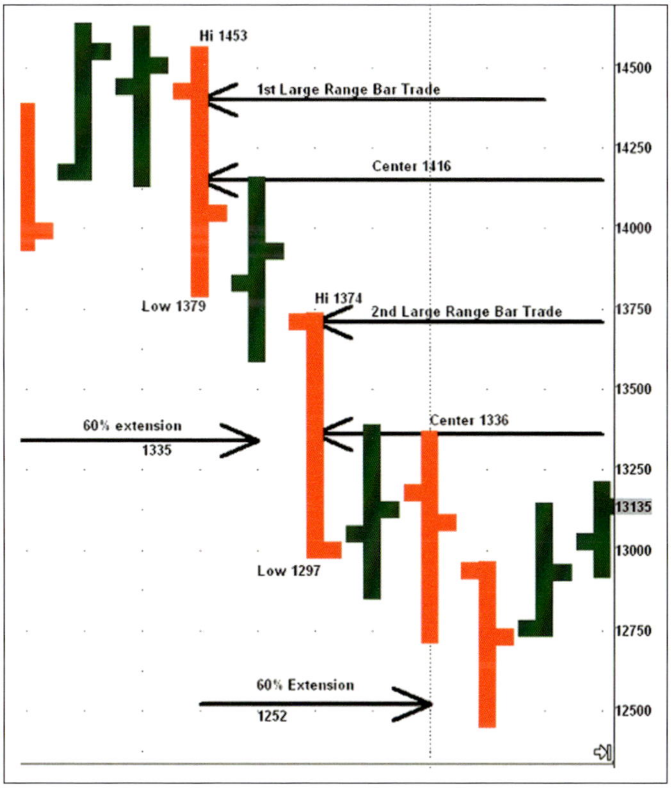

On the reversal Chart 2 there are actually four reversal bars, but I pointed out only two of them, one standard reversal and one Pinocchio reversal.

The difference between the two is that the standard reversal, after making a lower low, closed above the close of the preceding bar.

The Pinocchio also made a lower low, managed to close in the upper half of its range, and left a large portion of the range below the close—reminiscent of Pinocchio's long nose—but failed to close above the close of the previous bar.

Chart 2
Reversal Bars

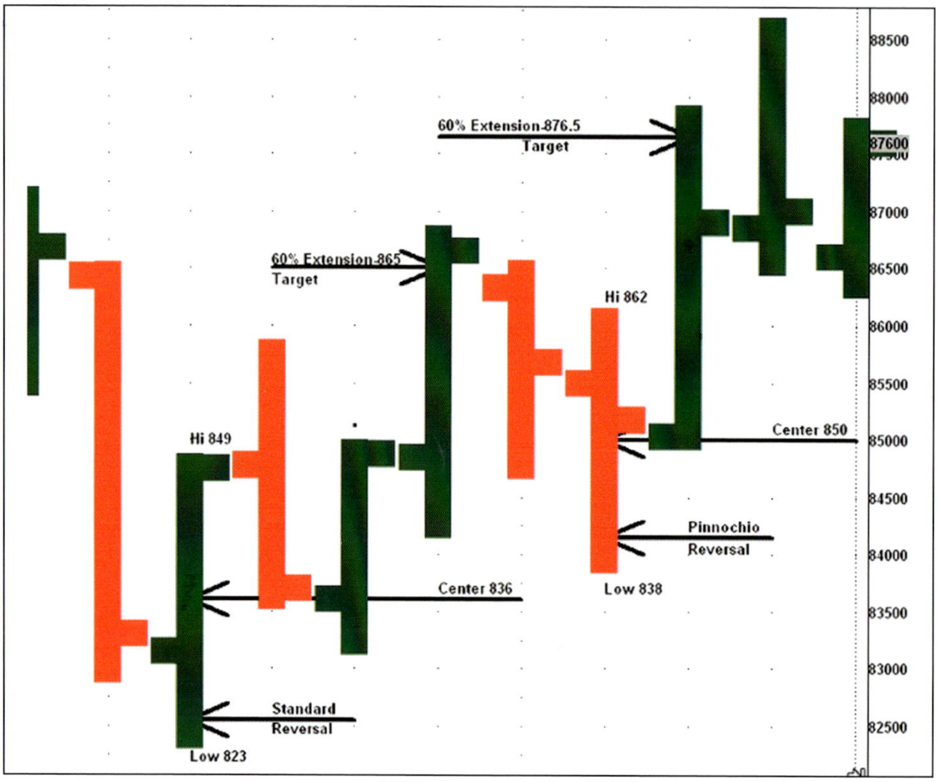

© 2009 eSignal. A division of Interactive Data Corporation (NYSE: IDC).

Outside bars are handled in the same manner as the large-range and reversal bars. They are less likely to occur, and many times represent a confused market. Because of that they are often found near a trend change.

My approach to outside bars is less aggressive. In Chart 3, the outside bar is going against the existing trend. To take a short position in the middle of a large bar like that and against the trend would be a bit foolhardy because of the amount of risk and the confusion that accompanies outside bars. As you can see, the market tested the high of the outside bar but failed to break it. After two more bars, it finally broke the low and one bar later hit the target. I usually trade outside bars in the direction of the breakout and use a tight stop to control the risk.

Chart 3
Outside Bars

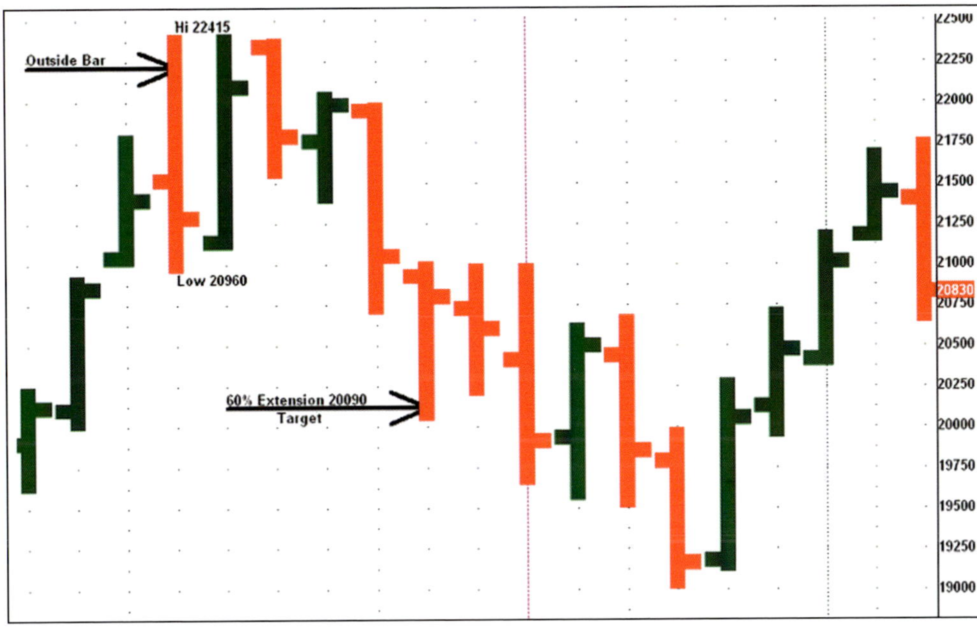

One final note:

Look at these charts and you will see that the center of virtually every bar is eventually revisited. The market seems to have a strong tendency to do that. As you study charts, it will benefit you to recognize the bars whose centers have not yet been revisited. Those centers can act as potential magnets that could eventually draw the market back to them.

12
Making It Work

I love a good cinnamon roll. In fact there aren't too many things in life that can beat a good cinnamon roll, as far as I'm concerned. In spite of that, sometimes I buy a cinnamon roll that disappoints at the very first bite. Other times a cinnamon roll will be pretty average. Once in a while, one will be pure ecstasy.

How can that be? After all, don't most bakeries use the same basic ingredients for a cinnamon roll? Of course they do. The problem must be with the way they combine those ingredients. The right combination can make all the difference—not only in baking but also in trading.

What I want to do is give you an example or two of how you might find a trade and then use the things we've talked about to turn it into a plan that has a good chance for success.

Chart 1 represents the movement of the S&P 500 over approximately thirty hours with each bar equal to one hour. I chose the S&P for discussion because it is a high volume, volatile, and popular market that trades almost around the clock.

To me, the most important thing to check is the direction of the 8 Period Averages. If they're up, the odds are best for a buy signal. If they're down, the odds favor the short side.

Next, it makes sense to be looking for buying opportunities if the market price has recently touched the bottom Bollinger Band or for selling opportunities when the market has touched or exceeded the top Bollinger Band. In these situations it is likely that the 8 Period Averages will not agree with the direction of the trade, so you need to look for other indicators to provide trade verification.

As we discuss these plans, remember that whatever applies to a buy signal will also apply to a sell signal except that the direction will be reversed. In the case of a market that has been to the bottom Bollinger Band recently, the first clue from a momentum indicator that it could be time to buy is when the 3 Period Exponential Average turns up, especially if the turn is sharp, like an elbow. On Chart 1, that happened on hour twelve for a buy and hours four and twenty-six for sells.

As soon as it turned up in hour twelve, I would place an order to buy at the middle of twelve's range (50 percent rule). Another valid buy entry would be to place a buy stop just above the high of hour twelve because, after touching the Bollinger Band, it violated the 8 Period Average and set up a shadow trade possibility.

Another positive in hour twelve was the 3 Period Exponential Average line crossing above the 5 Period Average line.

In hour thirteen, the 3 Average crossed up over the 8 Average and the 5 Average turned up. Those factors are continuing verification that the buy probabilities are improving.

At the end of hour thirteen, two more reasons for putting a buy stop above the current highs were added. There was a setup created for a trigger trade and also for a swing trade.

Hour fourteen let me in on my buy at 50 percent of hour twelve by trading down 60 percent of that period's range before starting back up. During hour fourteen, anyone planning to enter with a buy stop was rewarded by an entry, and if they were going for a quick 60 percent extension, they were all rewarded with a target hit as well.

At the end of hour fourteen, the 5 Period Averages crossed the 8 Period going up. The 20 Period Average is totally flat, which increases the odds that the market will continue to trade through it for an attempt at the top Bollinger Band. It would be tempting to try for an upper Bollinger target because the secondary shadow trade target is the upper Bollinger Band. It is also possible at this time to count back eight bars to find out that, in this case, an unchanged or higher close on bar 15 will be higher than seven, thereby turning the 8 Period Average up.

Bar 17 completed a power move to the upside, and 18 was the first reversal. That means that you should buy the opening of bar 19 because it's the bar after the first reversal in a power move. If you would rather, you could put a stop above bar 17 for another swing trade and take profit at a 60 percent, 100 percent, or 150 percent extension.

Bar 21 would have taken me out because it hit the second target for the shadow trade when it reached the price of the upper Bollinger Band. It also completed another legitimate power move, so bar 22 became the first reversal and 23 became another entry bar. Bar 22 also reached the middle of 21, which was a large-range bar, so the market could have been bought there. A buy stop above bar 21 would trigger another swing trade signal. Any time a swing trade is triggered, it is important to immediately bring a protective sell stop in below the low of the most recent reversal.

Bar 26 failed to reach any targets and all trades would have been stopped out.

Remember that our original idea was to look for buys after the bottom Bollinger Band and sell from the top Bollinger Band. It is possible to make winning trades by buying at the top Bollinger Band or vice versa, but the odds don't favor it. The power move trade would have a minor loss and the swing trade quite a bit more, but still a controllable amount.

Chart 2 is the same market over the same time span with thirty-minute bars instead of one-hour bars, although the numbers apply to the first thirty- minute bar of each hour, and the second thirty minutes are the bars without numbers.

As you study the thirty-minute chart over the same period of time, you can see how it gives you earlier indications that you are "on track" while still waiting to enter based on the hourly chart.

For instance, by the second half of bar 12, the 3 and 5 Period Averages had crossed above the 8 Period Average and, in the first half of bar 13, the 8 Period Average turned up an hour and a half earlier and at a better price than the sixty-minute signal. These are all positive indications that should encourage you to take the trade.

Notice that on the thirty-minute chart the market came back and touched the 8 Period Average line three times, usually an excellent entry opportunity, before the first major correction. During that same time period the hourly chart did not touch the 8 Period Averages at all. Remember that the 20 Period Average was flat on the hourly chart, indicating the possibility that the market might continue to the top Bollinger Band. The thirty-minute chart gave a much stronger indication of that by showing the 20 Period Average lines in a strong upward trend.

Imagine the additional encouragement you could have received along the way by seeing the thirty-minute data verify the direction of the market and validity of your decisions as the trade progressed. Also, the shorter-term chart gave you additional opportunities to add to the original position each time it touched the 8 Period Averages.

Chart 1

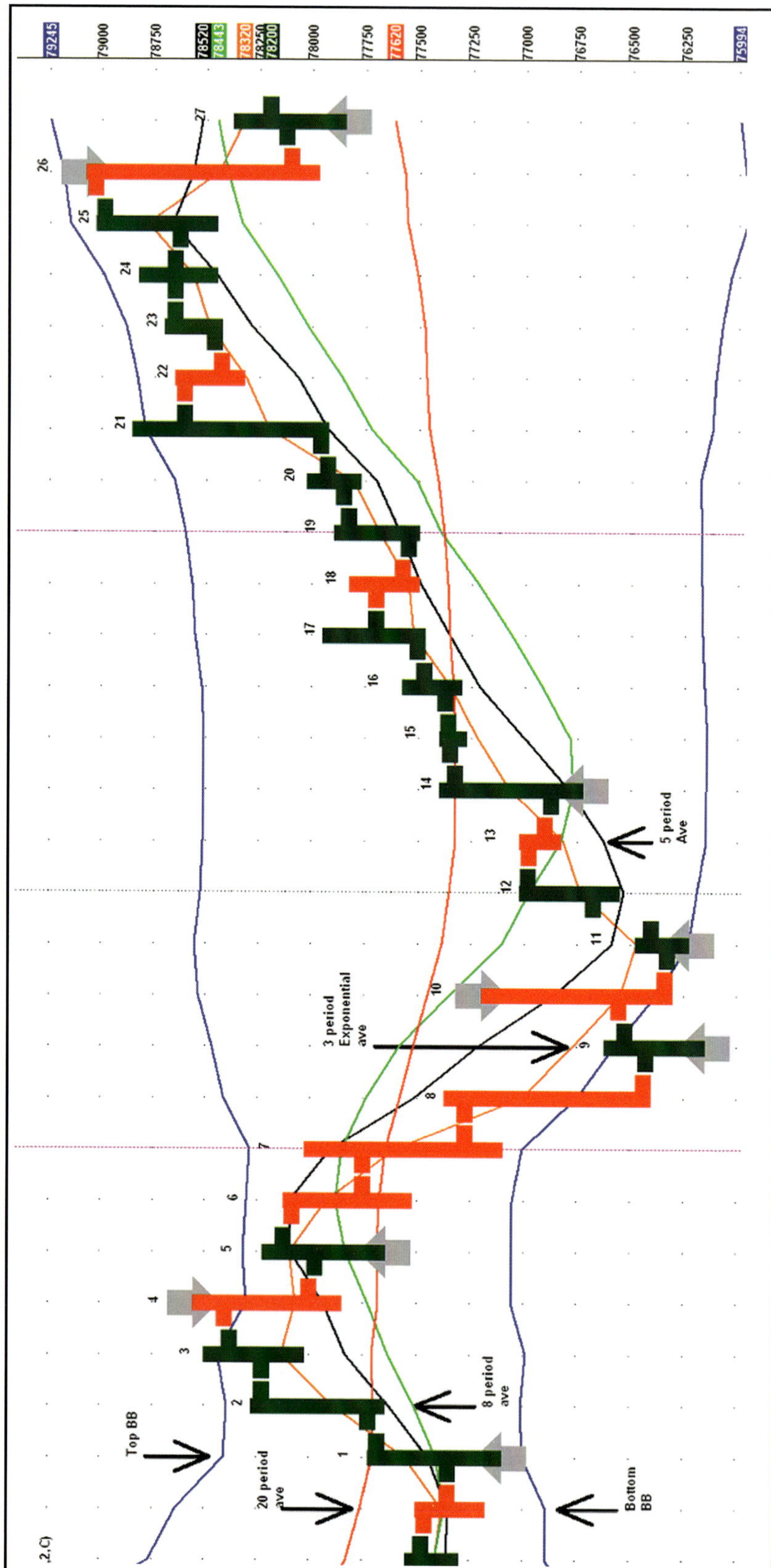
79245
79000
78750
78520
78443
78320
78250
78200
78000
77750
77620
77500
77250
77000
76750
76500
76250
75994
Top BB
20 period ave
8 period ave
Bottom BB
3 period Exponential ave
5 period Ave

Chart 2

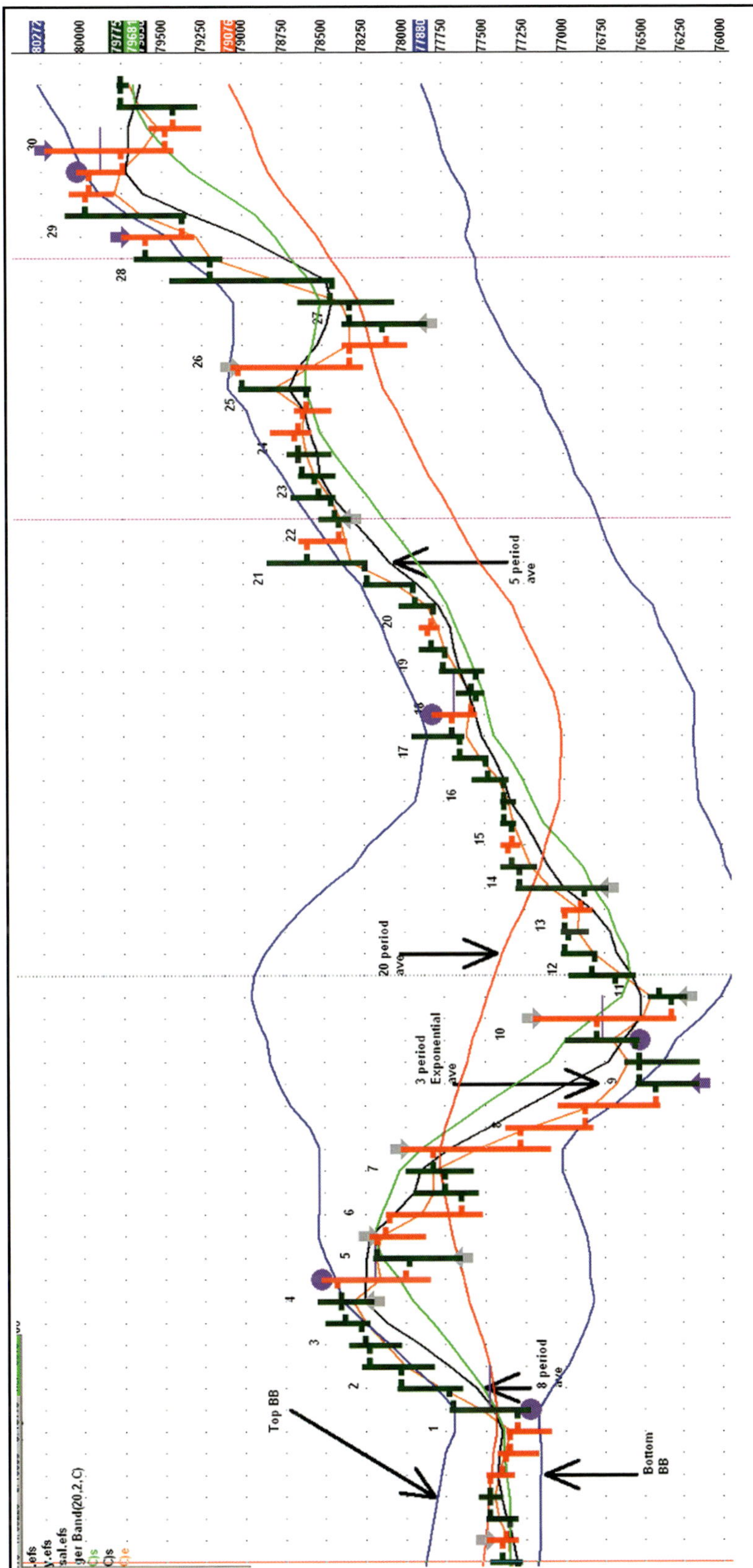
Top BB
Bottom BB
8 period ave
3 period Exponential ave
20 period ave
5 period ave

Common Mistakes Traders Make

There are three major mistakes that plague most traders. First, the protective stops on trades are placed in the wrong places, resulting in either too much risk or not enough. Too much risk takes more of the trading equity than it should when the trade doesn't work and makes it much more difficult to come back to a positive balance. Not enough risk frequently takes the trader out of a trade before the goal is attained. As a result, a winning trade is replaced by a small loss, no loss, or a less than an adequate gain.

The second mistake many traders make is failing to have a plan in case the trade goes bad, so no protective stop is used at all. I know that almost everyone thinks they can just get out if they don't like the trade. Therefore there is no need for an automated exit (that's another way to say protective stop). I would suggest that almost no one can "just get out" once they are caught in a losing trade.

As a boy I knew several farmers in our small neighborhood who were missing one of their hands. One of them was a family friend, and out of curiosity I asked him how it had happened. He told me that while he was picking corn one day, an excessive number of husks and stalks collected between the rollers on the machine so that it couldn't snap the ears of corn from the stalks. Since this had been a persistent problem and he was tired of dealing with it, he decided to save some time by letting the corn picker continue to run while he cleaned the extra debris out of the rollers.

As he grabbed some corn stalks to pull them out, the rollers caught them and started to pull them through. He told me that in retrospect he believes he had plenty of time to let go of the stalks, but his instincts took over and, instead of releasing the debris, he tightened his grip and was pulled into the machine.

Just as that farmer couldn't let go of the corn stalks even though he knew he should, I would suggest that almost no one can "just get out" once they are caught in a losing trade—even though they know they should—unless they have already put an automatic exit in place.

There is something inherently ingrained in most of us that makes us resist letting go of something we've worked on. I have watched good trading friends lose ridiculous amounts of money for no reason except that they couldn't turn loose a loser. Most of the trading methods we've discussed in this book have a built in risk point, but if you can't find a good technical place to carry a protective stop, at least assign a dollar amount to the risk side of the trade and put the stop in.

The third mistake comes from the misguided notion that winning is easy and knowing how to deal with loss is the most important thing in trading.

It is important to know how to deal with loss, but I will submit that knowing how to deal with winning is more important. The foolishness surrounding victory has blindsided even the best of us at some time in our careers. Because we aren't looking at the winning side for failure, it can walk right up and steal a fortune from us before we realize what happened.

We steal from ourselves because we fail to have a target, or even when we do, we don't stay in a trade long enough to reach the goal.

Trading Lies That Steal from You

One of the biggest lies in the trader's world is a line that we've all heard, **"You can't go broke taking a profit."**

It sickens me every time I hear someone say that because taking a profit is frequently precisely what breaks traders.

Most traders will take the risk warnings to heart and faithfully calculate the risk/reward parameters before carefully placing their entry along with the perfect protective stop. That's great, but as soon as the trade is triggered, they begin to watch it closely and then start to question whether their reward calculations were accurate and finally entertain thoughts about how "some profit is better than no profit at all" (not).

Sometimes, shortly after entry, the market will dip down and approach the protective stop level before it turns and heads back up. In most of those cases, the trader bravely watches the market and leaves the stop alone because he understands that you must endure risk to play the game.

Once the stop has been tested and held and the market once again begins its ascent, our brave trader frequently gets the shakes and begins to say things like, "I don't want any cheese; I just want out of the trap." That's more bad trading philosophy. Do you see what is happening? Our trader has convinced himself that it's fine to take all of the risk but not necessary to take all of the profit. That is not only bad philosophy, it's bad math; and the math is what will beat you. Here's how.

Let's say that you plan to make trades with a 2-to-1 reward/risk ratio and you are confident you can win 50 percent of your trades. Great plan! Now let's say that "because some profit is better than no profit" and "you can't go broke taking a profit," you end up getting out of most of your trades early, but you still win 50 percent of the trades and on average gain as much as you lose.

At least you are breaking even, except for just a couple of minor details. Do you pay commissions? Do you experience any slippage? What happens if you ever have a losing streak? The commission costs alone will sink your boat. If you don't stay for the profits you deserve, there will be a host of other things to eventually take a toll you can't afford. You can't afford to cheat yourself!

While we're talking about cheating ourselves, let's discuss another problem we all have from time to time that no one really wants to talk about. It's the inability to "pull the trigger."

This difficulty will be one of the most likely reasons for your demise if you fail as a trader.

Paper Trading vs. the Real Thing

For many of you it has been a challenge to reach this point in this book because we have been talking about things that were new to you and looking at markets from a different direction than you are used to. I'm proud of you for the tenacity and discipline you have shown. However, to make it all worthwhile, you will need to actually enter the trades, and that can be a greater challenge for some of you than you anticipated.

A lot of people test new concepts by paper trading (pretend trading). That makes good sense as long as the trader realizes there is a difference between paper and real trading.

In paper trading there is no emotion. No money is at risk and there are no profits to be taken, so it is relatively easy to place protective stops where they belong and hang in there until the profit target is reached. A totally different dynamic comes into play when real money is brought into the equation. The important thing to remember is that no system or plan can be successful unless it is activated.

Consistently good results will almost always track the following decision pattern:

1. Look for a trade setup.
2. Check to see if there are other types of indicators supporting or negating the validity of the trade setup you've found.
3. Assess the probabilities of success by finding a confluence of agreement from other indicators.
4. Calculate the risk/reward ratio and make sure the reward justifies the risk.
5. Enter the trade with your eyes wide open.
6. Place the protective stop and the profit target.

Follow that pattern consistently and understand before you start that no matter how good your method is there will be losing trades. It's a cost of doing business, and you cannot let that keep you from staying with your plan.

BE DISCIPLINED. BE BRAVE. TRADE WELL!

13

How to Place the Trade

For the first time trader, this entire process can seem a bit daunting. To make it easier for you, I will attempt to explain the basics of placing the orders to complete a trade. Let's say that we want to trade a market that is trending up. We'll call this market Gismo. We have been watching Gismo for a while, hoping it would pull back some and allow us to join the trend. So far, it has moved up 10 points from the recent low.

There are three basic ways to enter any market. The first way, and sloppiest, is to simply buy at the market. In this method, one would tell the broker to buy Gismo at the market. That means that you are willing to accept and will get the price that the market trades at when your order reaches the trading floor, which should be immediately.

You would then place a protective sell stop (see stop in the glossary) at the price you have chosen to set a limit on the risk. Let's say you bought Gismo at 7 and are willing to risk 3 points, so the sell stop would be at 4. You would then tell the broker to place a sell stop on Gismo at 4 and make it GTC (Good 'til Cancelled). That simply means that you want the protective stop to stay at 4 points until you say otherwise.

Now you need to place the order for your profit target. This will be a priced order, meaning that it will state a price at which you hope to take profit. Since the risk is 3 points, the minimum point of profit should be at least twice as much, or 6 points. Using that as our profit objective, we'll add 6 points to the entry price of 7 for a target price of 13. Tell the broker to place an order to sell Gismo at 13, GTC. Now the trade is set. Adjustments will come later.

The second way to enter the market is to buy it using a priced order. Since Gismo recently moved up 10 points and markets frequently pull back about 50 percent, let's buy a 5 point pull back (one-half of 10 points). Now we are in at 5 instead of 7. We could still risk 3 points and place the protective stop at 2. Tell the broker to place a sell stop on Gismo at 2, GTC.

Since there is no reason that the profit target should change, you now have a 3 point risk but an 8 point profit potential. Tell the broker to place a sell order on Gismo at 13, GTC.

The third way to enter the Gismo market is to use a buy stop. A buy stop works just like the protective sell stop except that this time the stop will put you into the market rather than out of the market. Since 10 is the recent high price in Gismo, let's put a buy stop at 11 so that we will only buy Gismo if it has enough strength to recover from the pull back and begin to make higher prices. Tell your broker to place a buy stop on Gismo at 11, GTC.

If you use this method of entry, the profit target will need to be moved up, and you will probably need to make adjustments to the protective stop price as well. It is important to maintain a reasonable risk/reward ratio, and that should be a factor in determining whether or not to use this method. Once the buy stop has been reached, follow the same procedure in placing the protective sell stop and the priced sell order.

Let's say you bought Gismo at 5 points and it began to trade higher. If it were to trade above 10 points, which was the previous high, it might make sense to move your protective stop up. That way you could reduce or eliminate the risk. Tell your broker to cancel your protective sell stop on Gismo at 2 points and replace it with a sell stop at 5 points. This type of order is called a cancel/replace. Now, if Gismo comes back down before it reaches the profit target, the protective stop should take you out at 5 points, where you got in.

Glossary of Terms

Bar—A vertical line drawn on a chart or graph that represents a particular quantity of time. The bar will indicate the first price, high, low, and last price of that segment of time.

Bollinger Bands—This technical analysis tool was invented by John Bollinger and is typically used to measure when prices could be considered to be abnormally high or low. It consists of three bands, the upper and lower (abnormal) being separated from the middle (normal) band by a standard deviation. The usual use of this tool is to determine when prices have stretched to a level so extreme that it should cause them to return to normal.

Breakout—Represents a situation where the market suddenly moves into a price level above or below a range that it has been trading in for some time.

Candlestick—Same as a bar except the portion of the price range between the first and last prices is expanded giving it the shape (body) of a candle. The remainder of the price range is the shadow.

Exponential Moving Average—Similar to a Simple Moving Average (see explanation below), except that more weight is given to the latest data.

Limit—An established price distance from the previous daily close beyond which the market is not allowed to trade. Many markets have removed limits in recent years because they interfere with the free flow of price movement.

Market Order—An order that indicates a willingness to accept whatever price is available when it arrives at the exchange.

Overbought—The subjective determination that a price has gone up too far, too fast and will not sustain that level.

Oversold—The subjective determination that a price has fallen too far, too fast and will not sustain that level.

Positions—Accumulate holdings in a designated market.

Priced Order—An order placed with the requirement that it be filled at that price or better.

Resistance—A price level above the market that could temporarily act as a ceiling.

Retracement—The process of a market trading back in the direction from which it came.

Simple Moving Average—Calculated by adding the closing price for a number of time periods and then dividing the total by that number of time periods. The movement is created by dropping the oldest price in the average and replacing it with the most recent price to arrive at a new average. Short-term averages respond more quickly to price changes than long-term averages.

Stop—A stop is a priced order that will not be activated until the market actually touches that price. At that time it becomes a market order and will be filled at the market as soon as possible. It allows you to place a buy order above the current market price or a sell order below the current price that will not be executed until the market gets there.

Support—A price level below the market that could temporarily act as a floor.

Tick—The minimum price movement.

Trend—The established direction of the market, either up, down, or sideways.

About the Author

Phil Storer began his trading career in the early 1970s and has continued to trade without interruption to the present time. A driving desire to win, a great dislike for loss, and a strong respect for patience and discipline have been the qualities that have helped him create success throughout the years. Although he has traded stocks for many years, he has always had a special love for commodities as another form of investment. Having grown up on a dairy farm, his close ties to the farming community gave him an "extra reason" early in his career to excel in that arena.

Although Phil stays current concerning the fundamental factors influencing the markets he is trading, he bases the decisions regarding entering and exiting trades almost exclusively on technical indicators. The simple, no-nonsense approaches that he uses have come from years of testing plans and methods for trading until only the most reliable are left. His suggestions for trading are consistently simple and contain a high degree of reliability because they are intended to cater to a working environment.

Phil works with speculative and hedging accounts, using tools that he has developed to outsmart the stock and futures markets. He specializes in providing custom-tailored plans and services that are efficient and effective. His willingness to work with traders' specific needs and desires is a major factor in his success. His prior experiences as a teacher, author, and college coach have helped Phil to effectively transfer his extensive knowledge of the markets to those who work with him.